PYTHON PROGRAMMING FOR BEGINNERS

The Complete Python Coding Crash Course.
Boost Your Growth with an Innovative Ultra-Fast Learning Framework and Exclusive Hands-On Interactive Exercises & Projects

2 in 1 Theory and Practice

by

codeprowess

Table of Contents

Thank you!

Creating this book represented a journey fueled by dedication and our deep-seated passion for disseminating knowledge and skills that are pivotal in navigating our rapidly evolving, dynamic world. Your involvement truly makes a significant difference and propels us forward in our quest to enrich and empower lives through education. Thank you for being an integral part of this journey!

Prior to getting started let's address a few essential steps:
1) Access Your Supplementary Materials: We strongly encourage you to take advantage of the valuable bonus content that accompanies this resource. These resources can facilitate and augment your comprehension throughout the entirety of the text. To access these supplementary materials, please refer to the designated section located at the end of the book titled "**Retrieve Your Bonus Content**."

2) Share your excitement about having our book in your hands by leaving a quick review, Your feedback is invaluable to us and others, we would greatly appreciate it. Providing a review is simple and straightforward, will not take more than 1 minute. Just scan QR code provided below. Feel free to express yourself in a way that suits you best! How to?

Option A: Create a brief video review showcasing the book.

Option B: Prefer not to be on camera? No issue at all. You can opt to capture some photographs of the book or write just a brief textual review. Your insights are crucial, as they not only recognize our efforts but also assist others in discovering this resource.

Please note, while providing a review is entirely optional, your feedback is extremely important and valuable for us.

Scan the QR code below to leave your review

Thank you so much, and here's to the start of a great journey!

Chapter 1: Introduction

_Brief History of Python

Welcome to your very first foray into Python programming! Before we dive into writing your first piece of Python code, it's important to understand the foundation upon which Python stands. That foundation is its history, a fascinating tale that begins decades ago. Not only will this give you a sense of Python's development over the years, but it also offers insights into why Python is the way it is today. Let's jump into the time machine!

The Genesis: Python's Humble Beginnings

In December 1989, a Dutch programmer named Guido van Rossum decided to embark on a project to create a new programming language. This decision was born out of frustration with the ABC language, a teaching language he had been involved in developing at the Centrum Wiskunde & Informatica (CWI) in the Netherlands. While ABC had its merits, it fell short in many aspects. Guido envisioned a language that maintained the readability of ABC but offered more flexibility and functionality. Thus, Python was conceived.

Why the Name Python?

You might be wondering: what does a snake have to do with programming? Fun fact: Python is not named after the snake. Guido was a fan of the British comedy show "Monty Python's Flying Circus," and he wanted a name that was unique, fun, and a bit irreverent. So, Python it was!

Python's First Appearance

Python made its first public appearance as Python 0.9.0 in February 1991. This initial version already demonstrated Python's commitment to code readability and ease-of-use, featuring constructs like exception handling and functions. While it was still a far cry from the Python we know today, this release marked a promising start.

Python 1.0: Setting the Stage

Python 1.0 was released in 1994, featuring capabilities like lambda, map, filter, and reduce functions, which provided functional programming capabilities. It was a big step forward but still had room for improvement.

Python 2.x: The Era of Improvement

The next major milestone came in the form of Python 2.0, released in October 2000. With the introduction of list comprehensions, garbage collection, and Unicode support, Python became more powerful and efficient. This version also brought about the Python Software Foundation (PSF), a non-profit organization that took over Python's intellectual property from CWI, providing a robust organizational backing to Python.

Python 3.x: The Present and Future

The transition from Python 2 to Python 3, beginning in 2008, was a significant leap. Python 3 was not backward-compatible with Python 2, a risky move that nevertheless paid off. With features like a new syntax for print statements and integer division, as well as the introduction of new standard libraries, Python 3 set the stage for modern Python development.

Why Choose Python: Advantages and Use-Cases

Welcome to the world of Python! In the last sub-chapter, you got a dose of Python's fascinating history. But knowing the history is just a small part of the picture. You're probably eager to roll up your sleeves and dive into coding. But wait a minute. Why choose Python in the first place? There are many programming languages out there: Java, C++, Ruby, and the list goes on. So why is Python the right choice for you?

Universality and Versatility

Let's start with the basics. Python is a general-purpose programming language, which means it can be used for pretty much anything. Need to build a website? Python can do it. What about analyzing a huge dataset for your graduate thesis? Python has you covered. Developing a video game? Yes, Python is up for that as well. Its versatility makes it a one-stop-shop for a broad range of applications, and that's a huge plus.

Easy to Learn, Easy to Read

If you're a beginner or even if you've dabbled in other languages, Python offers ease of learning that is second to none. The syntax is simple and incredibly readable. Unlike languages that are filled with brackets and semicolons, Python uses indentation to define code blocks. This makes your code clean, organized, and easy on the eyes. You'll spend less time debugging and more time actually coding.

A Thriving Community and Loads of Resources

Let's be honest; learning to code can be tough. But it becomes much easier when you have a supportive community and a plethora of resources to guide you. Python's community is enormous and continually growing. You'll find numerous forums, online courses, and books dedicated to Python programming. Plus, if you're ever in a jam, a quick Google search will likely lead you to someone who has faced the same issue.

Libraries and Frameworks

The abundance of libraries and frameworks is another feather in Python's cap. Whether it's data manipulation through Pandas, scientific computing with NumPy, or data visualization using Matplotlib, Python has libraries for virtually anything you'd want to do. Frameworks like Django make web development a breeze. You're not just writing code from scratch; you're standing on the shoulders of giants.

Data Science and Machine Learning

The rise of data science, artificial intelligence (AI), and machine learning has also contributed to Python's popularity. Python has become the go-to language for these emerging fields, thanks to specialized libraries like TensorFlow, Keras, and Scikit-Learn. With Python, you're future-proofing your skillset.

Application in Various Industries

From tech giants like Google and Facebook to NASA, Python is everywhere. It is not limited to one industry or sector. Finance, healthcare, telecommunications—Python has made its mark everywhere. The versatility and capabilities of Python make it an industry favorite.

Rapid Development and Prototyping

Python's clean and straightforward syntax makes for quicker development and prototyping. This saves not just time but also costs for businesses and individual developers. Time-to-market is crucial in today's competitive environment, and Python gives you that edge.

Cross-Platform Compatibility

Write once, run anywhere—that's the Python philosophy. Python is cross-platform, meaning you can run your Python script on any operating system without a hitch. This is especially handy if you're developing applications that need to be used across different platforms.

Strong Support for Integration

Python plays well with others. Whether you need to integrate your Python application with a web service or invoke C/C++ libraries, Python has tools to let you do that smoothly. Its strong integration capabilities make it a flexible and powerful choice for any project.

Automation and Scripting

Last but not least, Python is a strong choice for automation and scripting tasks. Many system administrators use Python to write scripts that help them automate various administrative tasks. You don't need to write hundreds of lines of code for a simple script, a few lines of Python will usually do the trick.

Safety and Error Handling

While Python does many things right, it's crucial to know that no programming language is without its pitfalls. Python's dynamic typing system can sometimes be a double-edged sword, leading to runtime errors that could have been caught at the compilation stage in statically-typed languages. However, Python has robust error handling features like `try`, `except`, and `finally` blocks that allow you to catch and gracefully handle exceptions.

Practical Exercises

1. List down five project ideas that you'd like to develop. Consider the advantages of Python as described in this sub-chapter. Would Python be a suitable choice for these projects? Why or why not?
2. Research and find three Python libraries or frameworks that interest you. What do they do, and how could they be useful in your coding journey?

Setting Up Your Python Development Environment

Hey there, future Pythonista! Now that you're convinced Python is the way to go, let's set up your Python development environment. Trust me, it's easier than assembling a piece of IKEA furniture, and I'll guide you through each step. Setting up a solid development environment can make your coding journey smooth, efficient, and, believe it or not, more enjoyable.

Why a Development Environment Matters

First, let's chat about why this is important. Imagine trying to paint a masterpiece without a proper canvas or the right shades of paint. Your development environment is your canvas; it's where you'll write, test, and run your code. A well-configured environment ensures you can focus on coding rather than troubleshooting pesky errors.

Downloading and Installing Python

Alright, let's get our hands dirty. The first thing you need to do is download Python.

→ Python's Official Setup Guide https://www.python.org/downloads

Windows

1. Visit the Python Official Website
2. Download the latest Python installer for Windows. At the time of writing, it's Python 3.9.6.
3. Run the installer, and make sure you check the box that says "Add Python to PATH."

macOS

For Mac users, Python 2.7 comes pre-installed, but we need Python 3.x. To install it, you can use Homebrew. Open Terminal and type `brew install python3`.

Alternatively, you can download the macOS installer from the Python Official Website.

Linux

Most Linux distributions come with Python pre-installed. To check which version you have, open a terminal and type `python3 --version`.

If it's not installed, use your package manager to install Python 3.x.

IDEs and Text Editors

You'll need something to write your code in. The basic Notepad or TextEdit could technically work, but they won't make your life easier. You need an Integrated Development Environment (IDE) or a specialized text editor.

Popular Choices

1. PythonIdle typically comes directly installed with python. You can find it among your apps

IDLE (**Python** 3.1

1. PyCharm: A feature-rich IDE with excellent debugging capabilities and plugin support.
2. Visual Studio Code (VS Code): A lightweight, open-source editor with strong Python support.
3. Jupyter Notebook: Ideal for data science and machine learning projects, it allows you to include text, code, and visuals in the same document.

Choose the one that resonates with you. Most of these editors come with step-by-step installation guides, so you shouldn't have any issues there.

Installing Essential Packages

Please follow the instruction directly from the python.org site for a detailed guide as depending on your environment instructions may be different, <u>please pay attention and select the Operating System you're a using to see the correct instructions</u> (Unix/macOS or Windows)

<u>https://packaging.python.org/en/latest/tutorials/installing-packages/</u>

High level these are the steps to follow:

1. There are some packages that you'll find yourself using frequently. Let's install some essentials to get you started.
3. Use the package manager pip to install: `pip -m install numpy pandas matplotlib`.
4. Congrats, you've just installed your first Python packages!

Virtual Environments

Before you ask, no, we're not entering the Matrix. A virtual environment is an isolated space where you can install packages without affecting the global Python setup on your machine.

Creating a Virtual Environment

Please follow the instruction directly from the python.org site for a detailed guide as depending on your environment instructions may be different, <u>please pay attention and select the Operating System you're a using to see the correct instructions</u>. Here is the anchored link:

<u>https://packaging.python.org/en/latest/tutorials/installing-packages/#creating-virtual-environments</u>

High level these are the steps to follow:

1. Open a terminal or command prompt.
2. Navigate to the folder where you want your Python project to live.
3. Type `py -m venv myenv` to create a new environment named `myenv`.
4. Now, every time you work on your project, activate the virtual environment. This will ensure that any packages you install won't interfere with other projects.

You can also find more info here:
<u>https://packaging.python.org/en/latest/guides/installing-using-pip-and-virtual-environments/</u>

Safety and Error Handling

1. Setting up a development environment is generally low-risk, but there are a few precautions to take.
2. Permissions: Make sure you have the necessary permissions to install software on your machine.
3. Check Version Compatibility: Before installing packages, check if they're compatible with your Python version.
Beware of Third-Party Installers: Always download software from trusted sources to avoid malware.

Practical Exercises

1. Install Python and set up a virtual environment. Install a package of your choice and run a sample program to check if everything is functioning as it should.

2. Experiment with different IDEs or text editors. Which one do you find most comfortable for your workflow, and why?

Chapter 2: Your First Steps in Python

Writing Your First Python Program

Hello, again! Ready to write your first Python program? I promise, it's not going to be a snooze-fest. Think of this as your first ride on a bicycle. A bit wobbly at first, but soon you'll be cruising!

Why Your First Program Matters

Let's get one thing straight: your first program is a big deal. It's that first brushstroke on a blank canvas, the foundation of the skyscraper you'll eventually build. It teaches you the syntax, the rules of the road, and gives you a taste of the sweet victory that is running a successful program.

The Iconic "Hello, World!"

Tradition dictates that the first program you write in any programming language should display the text "Hello, World!" to the screen. Let's uphold this time-honored ritual.

Step 1: Open Your IDE or Text Editor

Open the IDE or text editor you installed in the last chapter. Got it open? Great!

Step 2: Create a New Python File

In your IDE, create a new Python file and name it something memorable like `hello_world.py`. The `.py` extension is crucial; it tells the computer that this is a Python file.

Step 3: Write the Code

In your new Python file, type the following code:

```python
print("Hello, World!")
```

Just that one line! Python is refreshingly simple, isn't it?

Step 4: Save and Run

Save the file and then run it. If everything's set up correctly, your screen should display:

```
Hello, World!
```

Jump for joy, do a little dance— you've just written and run your first Python program!

Understanding Your First Program

Let's break down what you just did:

- `print()`: This is a function that tells Python to perform an action. In this case, it's to display whatever is inside the parentheses.
- `"Hello, World!"`: This is a string, a series of characters enclosed in quotes.

The `print()` function takes the string and pushes it to your screen. Simple, but effective.

Common Mistakes and How to Avoid Them

Since this is a pretty straightforward task, the chances of messing up are slim. However, here are some things to watch out for:

- **Syntax Errors**: Forgetting quotes around the string or mistyping `print` will result in errors.
- **File Extension**: Make sure the file is saved with a `.py` extension.
- **Environment**: Ensure you're running the code in a Python environment.

Your Next Simple Programs

Don't stop at "Hello, World!" Here are a couple more basic programs to try:

Display Your Name

```
print("My name is [Your Name]")
```

Replace `[Your Name]` with your actual name, save, and run.

A Simple Calculator

```
print("Sum of 5 and 3 is:", 5+3)
```

Save and run this program to see how Python performs addition right inside the `print()` function.

Interactive Greeting

```
name = input("What's your name? ")
print(f"Hello, {name}!")
```

This program asks for your name and greets you personally.

Practical Exercises

1. Write a program that prints out "Good Morning, [Your Name]!".
2. Write another program that multiplies two numbers and displays the result.

_ Understanding Variables and Data Types

Engaging Introduction

Hey there, coding enthusiasts! So you've just written your first Python program. Awesome, right? Now that you've gotten your feet wet, it's time to dive a little deeper. In this chapter, we'll talk about variables and data types in Python, two foundational concepts that you'll use in every program you write. Buckle up, because this is where it gets interesting!

Learning Objectives

- Understand what variables are and how to create them
- Learn about the different data types in Python
- Know how to use variables in calculations and operations

What are Variables?

In simple terms, variables are like containers where you can store information. Think of them as boxes in your attic or jars on your kitchen shelf, holding various items for future use. In programming, these "items" can be numbers, text, or more complex types of data.

How to Create Variables

Creating a variable in Python is a piece of cake. It's so straightforward that it doesn't even require a special command. You simply write the variable name, followed by the equals sign (=), and then the value you want to store.

```
name = "John"
age = 30
height = 6.1  # height in feet (1.85 meters)
```

The above example declares three variables:
- `name` holds the text "John"
- `age` contains the number 30
- `height` stores the floating-point number 6.1

The = sign is called the "assignment operator." It doesn't mean "equal to" like in math; instead, it means "assign the value on the right to the variable on the left."

Rules for Naming Variables

1. Must start with a letter or an underscore.
2. Can contain letters, numbers, and underscores.
3. Are case-sensitive.

Good Examples: `myVariable`, `_temp`, `AGE`
Bad Examples: `1var`, `my-variable`, `For`

Understanding Data Types

Python has various data types, and understanding them is crucial for effective programming. Let's take a look at the most common types you'll come across:
- **Integers**: Whole numbers like 1, 7, 352, -5.
- **Floats**: Decimal numbers like 3.14, 2.71, 0.99.
- **Strings**: Text enclosed in quotes, e.g., "Hello, World!", "Python", "42".
- **Booleans**: True or False values, used for conditional statements.

You don't need to explicitly define a variable's data type; Python does that automatically. For example:

```
integer_example = 5  # This is an integer
float_example = 3.14  # This is a float
string_example = "Hello, World!"  # This is a string
boolean_example = True  # This is a boolean
```

Type Conversion

Sometimes you'll need to convert between these types, which Python makes super easy. Let's say you have an integer, and you need it to be a string:

```
age = 30  # Integer
age_as_string = str(age)  # Now it's a string
```

Safety and Error Handling

Be cautious when performing type conversion. Not all types can be easily converted. For example, converting a string with text to an integer will result in an error:

```
bad_conversion = int("hello")  # This will throw an error
```

Be mindful of this to avoid unnecessary hiccups in your code.

Practical Exercises

1. Create a variable called my_name and assign your name to it.
2. Create another variable called my_age and assign your age to it.
3. Multiply my_age by 2 and store the result in a new variable called double_age.

Solutions

```
my_name = "Your Name"
my_age = Your Age
double_age = my_age * 2
```

Basic Operators

Hello again, future Python masters! So, you've gotten to know variables and data types pretty well by now. But what's the point of storing all this data if we can't do anything with it, right? That's where operators come in. Operators help us perform operations on our variables, like adding numbers or combining text. Let's dive in!

Learning Objectives

- Understand different types of operators in Python
- Learn how to perform basic operations on variables
- Get acquainted with operator precedence

Arithmetic Operators

Let's kick things off with arithmetic operators, the backbone of any calculation in Python. Here's what you need to know:

Addition (+)

```
result = 3 + 4  # result is 7
```

Subtraction (-)

```
result = 10 - 3   # result is 7
```

Multiplication (*)

```
result = 4 * 5   # result is 20
```

Division (/)

```
result = 8 / 2   # result is 4.0
```

Notice that the result is a float (4.0), not an integer (4).

Floor Division (//)

```
result = 9 // 2   # result is 4
```

This gives the quotient without the remainder, as an integer.

Modulus (%)

```
result = 9 % 2   # result is 1
```

This gives the remainder of the division.

Exponentiation (**)

```
result = 3 ** 2   # result is 9
```

Raises 3 to the power of 2.

Arithmetic operators work with variables just as well:

```
a = 5
b = 2
addition = a + b   # result is 7
```

Comparison Operators

Comparison operators help us make decisions in our code by comparing values. Here's a list of them:

Equal to (==)

```
5 == 5   # True
```

Not equal to (!=)

```
5 != 4   # True
```

Greater than (>)

```
5 > 4   # True
```

Less than (<)

```
4 < 5   # True
```

Greater than or equal to (>=)

```
5 >= 5   # True
```

Less than or equal to (<=)

```
4 <= 5   # True
```

Logical Operators

Logical operators are used to combine conditional statements:

AND (and)

```
(5 > 4) and (3 > 2)   # True
```

OR (or)

```
(5 > 4) or (2 > 3)   # True
```

NOT (not)

```
not (5 > 4)   # False
```

Operator Precedence

Understanding operator precedence is crucial to avoid mistakes in your calculations. For example, multiplication and division are performed before addition and subtraction. When in doubt, use parentheses to ensure the correct order of operations.

```
# Without parentheses
result = 3 + 4 * 2   # result is 11
```

```
# With parentheses
result = (3 + 4) * 2   # result is 14
```

Safety and Error Handling

Be cautious when dividing by zero or working with incompatible data types. Python will throw errors for these, and it's good to anticipate them.

```
# This will throw an error
result = 5 / 0
```

Practical Exercises

Create variables `a = 5` and `b = 2`. Calculate `a + b`, `a - b`, `a * b`, and `a / b` and store these in separate variables.

1. Use comparison operators to check if `a` is greater than `b`, and store the result in a variable called `is_a_greater`.

2. Combine logical operators to check if `a` is greater than `b` and `a` is an even number. Store the result in a variable called `complex_condition`.

Solutions

1. `a = 5 b = 2 addition = a + b subtraction = a - b multiplication = a * b division = a / b`
2. `is_a_greater = a > b`
3. `complex_condition = (a > b) and (a % 2 == 0)`

Numbers in Python: Mastering Mathematical Functions

Alright, you've gotten the basics down. You know how to create variables, how to use basic operators, but what about those special mathematical functions? Don't worry, Python's got your back. Let's dive right in and explore functions that will give you a numerical edge (pun intended) in Python!

Learning Objectives:

- Understand and use various Python built-in functions related to numbers.
- Learn about mathematical libraries and their utility.
- Gain practical insights through examples.

Abs Function

Step 1: Understanding `abs()`

The `abs()` function is like your trustworthy GPS for numbers. It points you to the positive side of the numerical world by returning the absolute value of a number. Simply put, it turns negative numbers into positive ones.

```
# Example
print(abs(-42))   # Output: 42
```

Step 2: Safety Tips

This function takes integers and floats. Don't throw in other data types unless you're looking for trouble (or a TypeError).

Ceil Function

Step 1: Getting to Know `ceil()`

Part of Python's `math` library, `ceil()` rounds off a floating-point number UP to the nearest integer. Remember, you have to `import math` first.

```
import math
# Example
print(math.ceil(42.1))   # Output: 43
```

Step 2: Safety Tips

Since `ceil()` is in the `math` library, always remember to import it. Also, it only takes floats and integers as arguments.

Max Function and Min Function

Step 1: The Champions `max()` and `min()`

These functions take any number of arguments and return the highest and lowest value, respectively.

```
# Example
print(max(1, 42, 3))   # Output: 42
print(min(1, 42, 3))   # Output: 1
```

Step 2: Safety Tips

You can feed these functions both floats and integers, but make sure to compare apples with apples. Mixing data types like strings and numbers can result in a TypeError.

Pow Function

Step 1: The Powerhouse `pow()`

This one is straightforward. It takes two arguments, `x` and `y`, and returns `x` raised to the power of `y`.

```
# Example
print(pow(2, 3))   # Output: 8
```

Step 2: Safety Tips

Again, only floats and integers should be used as arguments.

Sqrt Function

Step 1: The Root Finder `sqrt()`

Another member of the `math` family, `sqrt()` returns the square root of a number. Don't forget to `import math`.

```
import math
# Example
print(math.sqrt(16))   # Output: 4.0
```

Step 2: Safety Tips

Only non-negative numbers allowed! Negative numbers will result in a `ValueError`.

Random Function and Randrange Function

Step 1: The Luck Generators `random()` and `randrange()`

These two functions from the `random` library generate random numbers. `random()` gives you a random float between 0 and 1, while `randrange()` gives you a random integer between the start and stop arguments.

22

```
import random
# Example
print(random.random())
print(random.randrange(1, 10))
```

Step 2: Safety Tips
Always remember to import the random library. And know that randrange() can throw a ValueError if the range is empty.

Sin, Cos, Tan Functions
Step 1: The Trigonometric Trio
From the math library, these functions take an angle in radians and return the sine (sin), cosine (cos), and tangent (tan) values.

```
import math
# Example
print(math.sin(math.pi/2))   # Output: 1.0
```

Step 2: Safety Tips
These functions take only numbers as arguments and make sure the angles are in radians, not degrees.

Practical Exercises
- Create a program that calculates the absolute difference between two numbers.
- Write a program that finds the highest and lowest numbers in a list.
- Implement a function that takes a number and returns its square root.

Solutions

Certainly! Here are the solutions to the exercises proposed in the "Numbers in Python" subchapter.

Exercise 1: Create a program that calculates the absolute difference between two numbers.
```
def absolute_difference(num1, num2):
    return abs(num1 - num2)


# Testing the function
result = absolute_difference(-10, 5)
print(f"The absolute difference between -10 and 5 is: {result}")   # Output: 15
```

Exercise 2: Write a program that finds the highest and lowest numbers in a list.
```
def find_extremes(num_list):
```

```
        return max(num_list), min(num_list)


# Testing the function
highest, lowest = find_extremes([1, 42, 3, 7])
print(f"The highest number is: {highest}")    # Output: 42
print(f"The lowest number is: {lowest}")       # Output: 1
```

Exercise 3: Implement a function that takes a number and returns its square root.

First, import the `math` library to use the `sqrt` function.

```
import math


def find_sqrt(num):
    if num < 0:
        return "Square root of negative numbers is not supported."
    return math.sqrt(num)


# Testing the function
result = find_sqrt(16)
print(f"The square root of 16 is: {result}")   # Output: 4.0
```

Feel free to test these exercise solutions by running them in your Python environment. Remember, these are just starting points—part of the fun is tweaking and expanding on them as you gain more confidence with Python's number functions!

Formatting Numbers

Formatting numbers can be crucial, especially when you're presenting data to someone else. Python provides several ways to format numbers for better readability and presentation.

format() Function

The `format()` function allows you to format numbers in various ways, including controlling the number of decimal places, alignment, and other aspects.

```
print(format(123.4567, '.2f'))   # Output: "123.46"
```

Exercise 1: Format the number 12345.6789 to show only two decimal places.

Formatting Floating-Point Numbers

You can use the `format()` function to format floating-point numbers as well. The general syntax is `{:.Nf}`, where N is the number of decimal places.

```
print('{:.2f}'.format(123.456))   # Output: "123.46"
```

Exercise : Format the number 12.34567 to show three decimal places.

Formatting Numbers in Scientific Notation
When dealing with very large or very small numbers, you may prefer to use scientific notation.

```python
print('{:.2e}'.format(1234567890))    # Output: "1.23e+09"
```

Exercise: Format the number 0.000123456789 to show in scientific notation with 3 decimal places.

Inserting Commas
For large numbers, it can be helpful to insert commas as thousand separators.

```python
print('{:,}'.format(1234567890))    # Output: "1,234,567,890"
```

Exercise: Format the number 9876543210 to include commas as thousand separators.

Formatting Number as Percentages
To format numbers as percentages, you can use the % symbol.

```python
print('{:.1%}'.format(0.456))    # Output: "45.6%"
```

Exercise: Format the number 0.789 as a percentage with no decimal places.

Setting Alignment
You can also control the alignment of the formatted number.

```python
print('{:>10}'.format(123))    # Output: "       123"
```

Exercise: Right-align the number 12345 in a field of width 20.

Formatting Integers
You can use the d specifier to format integers.

```python
print('{:d}'.format(123))    # Output: "123"
```

Exercise: Use the d specifier to format the integer 6789.

Chapter 3: Strings in Python
Strings are as essential as they are versatile, used in almost every Python program you can think of. So let's get straight into it, shall we?

Counting Number of Characters Using len() Function
To find the length of a string in Python, use the len() function. For instance:

```
word = "Python"
print(len(word))   # Output: 6
```

Exercise 1: Use `len()` to find the length of your full name.

_ Creating Empty Strings

You can create an empty string like this:

```
empty_string = ""
```

Or like this:

```
another_empty_string = str()
```

Exercise 2: Create an empty string and print its type using `type()`.

_ Escape Sequences

Escape sequences like `\n` for a new line or `\t` for a tab can be handy:

```
print("Hello\nWorld")   # Output: Hello
                        #         World
```

Exercise 3: Write a string that uses escape sequences to display a quote within a quote.

_ String Concatenation

To combine strings, you simply add them:

```
print("Hello " + "World")   # Output: Hello World
```

Exercise 4: Concatenate your first and last names with a space in between.

_ String Repetition Operator (*)

To repeat a string, use the `*` operator:

```
print("Hi " * 3)   # Output: Hi Hi Hi
```

Exercise 5: Repeat the word "Python" five times, separated by dashes.

_ Membership Operators — in and not in

You can check for substrings like this:

```
print("Py" in "Python")   # Output: True
```

Or like this:

```
print("py" not in "Python")   # Output: True
```

Exercise 6: Check if the word "apple" contains the letter "p".

_ Accessing Individual Characters in a String

You can access individual characters using index notation:

```
print("Python"[2])   # Output: t
```

Exercise 7: Access the last character of your full name using negative indexing.

_ *Slicing Strings*

Slicing helps to extract a range of characters:

```
print("Python"[1:4])   # Output: yth
```

Exercise 8: Slice the string "Pythonista" to get the substring "onist".

_ *Everything in Python is an Object*

Even strings are objects, which means they have methods like `upper()` to convert them to uppercase.

```
print("Python".upper())   # Output: PYTHON
```

_ *Classes and Object – The First Look*

Strings are instances of the `str` class, allowing you to use various methods on them.

```
word = "Python"
print(word.lower())   # Output: python
```

Exercise 9: Use the `.title()` method to title-case the string "hello world".

_ *ASCII Characters*

Each character has an ASCII (American Standard Code for Information Interchange) value.

ord() and chr() Function

ord() function: To get the ASCII value of a character.

```
print(ord('A'))   # Output: 65
```

chr() function: To get the character from an ASCII value.

```
print(chr(65))   # Output: A
```

Exercise 10: Use `ord()` to find the ASCII value of the first letter of your name.

_ *Suppressing newline in print() Function*

You can suppress the newline character at the end of `print()` by specifying `end=""`.

```
print("Hello, ", end="")
print("World!")   # Output: Hello, World!
```

Specifying Separator in print() Function

You can specify the separator between multiple arguments in the `print()` function:

```
print("Hello", "World", sep="-")   # Output: Hello-World
```

String Comparison

Strings can be compared lexicographically:

```
print("apple" > "banana")   # Output: False
```

Strings are Immutable

Strings can't be changed once created. Any operation that seems to modify a string actually creates a new string.

```
word = "Python"
new_word = word.replace("P", "J")
print(new_word)   # Output: Jython
```

Formatting String Using the `format()` Function

The `format()` method helps to format strings:

```
print("Hello, {}".format("World"))   # Output: Hello, World
```

Exercise 11: Format a string to output your first and last name, separated by a space.

Testing Strings

`isalnum()` **method:** Check if all characters are alphanumeric.
`isalpha()` **method:** Check if all characters are alphabetic.
`isdigit()` **method:** Check if all characters are digits.
`islower()` **and** `isupper()` **method:** Check if all characters are in lower or upper case.
`isspace()` **method:** Check if all characters are whitespaces.

Searching and Replacing Strings

`find()` **method:** Find the index of the first occurrence of a substring.
`replace()` **method:** Replace occurrences of a substring with another substring.

Converting Strings

`lower()` **and** `upper()` **methods:** Convert string to lower or upper case.
`capitalize()` **and** `title()` **methods:** Capitalize the first character or each word.
`swapcase()` **method:** Swap the case of each character.
`strip()` **method:** Remove leading and trailing whitespaces.

Formatting Methods

`center()` **method:** Center-align the string.
`ljust()` **and** `rjust()` **methods:** Left-justify or right-justify the string.

Solutions to the Exercises

Exercise 1
Let' say your Name is John Doe

```
print(len("John Doe"))  # Output: 8
```

Exercise 2

```
empty_string = ""
print(type(empty_string))  # Output: <class 'str'>
```

Exercise 3

```
print("He said, \"Hello, World!\"")
```

Exercise 4
Let's say your first name is "John" and your last name is "Doe".

```
print("John" + " " + "Doe")  # Output: John Doe
```

Exercise 5

```
print("Python-" * 4 + "Python")  # Output: Python-Python-Python-Python-Python
```

Exercise 6

```
print("p" in "apple")  # Output: True
```

Exercise 7
Let's say your full name is "John Doe".

```
print("John Doe"[-1])  # Output: e
```

Exercise 8

```
print("Pythonista"[2:8])  # Output: thonis
```

Exercise 9

```
print("hello world".title())  # Output: Hello World
```

Exercise 10
Let's say the first letter of your name is "J".

```
print(ord("J"))  # Output: 74
```

Exercise 11

Let's say your first name is "John" and your last name is "Doe".

```python
print("Hello, {} {}".format("John", "Doe"))  # Output: Hello, John Doe
```

Chapter 4: Diving into Data Structures

List and Tuples

You've just conquered the basics of Python programming. Now, let's jump into one of Python's power-houses: data structures. Specifically, we'll explore Lists and Tuples—two types of collections that can hold multiple items.

Lists in Python

In the Python universe, a list is an ordered collection of items, which means the order of the items matters. Lists are super versatile; you can store different types of elements such as integers, strings, other lists, and more. They are declared with square brackets [], and items are separated by commas.

Creating Lists

Let's create a list, shall we?

```
# Creating a list
my_list = [1, 2, 3, 'apple', 'banana']
print(my_list)  # Output: [1, 2, 3, 'apple', 'banana']
```

Yes, you read it right! Lists can store mixed types. But it's usually a good idea to store similar types of items for easier manipulation.

Accessing Elements

To access elements in a list, you use the index, starting with 0 for the first element.

```
# Accessing an element in a list
print(my_list[0])  # Output: 1
print(my_list[3])  # Output: 'apple'
Watch out! Python throws an IndexError if you try to access an index that doesn't exist.
```

Modifying Lists

Lists are mutable, which means you can change them after you've created them. For example:

```
# Modifying a list
my_list[0] = 'one'
print(my_list)  # Output: ['one', 2, 3, 'apple', 'banana']
```

List Operations

You can perform various operations with lists like append(), remove(), insert(), and more.

```
# Adding an element to the list
my_list.append('grapes')
print(my_list)  # Output: ['one', 2, 3, 'apple', 'banana', 'grapes']
```

31

```
# Removing an element from the list
my_list.remove('banana')
print(my_list)    # Output: ['one', 2, 3, 'apple', 'grapes']
```

Tuples in Python

While lists are cool, sometimes you want something a bit more permanent. That's where tuples come in. Unlike lists, tuples are immutable; once you create them, you can't change them.

Creating Tuples

Tuples are defined by enclosing the items in parentheses ():

```
# Creating a tuple
my_tuple = (1, 2, 3, 'apple', 'banana')
print(my_tuple)    # Output: (1, 2, 3, 'apple', 'banana')
```

Accessing Elements

Just like lists, you can access tuple elements by index:

```
# Accessing an element in a tuple
print(my_tuple[0])    # Output: 1
print(my_tuple[3])    # Output: 'apple'
```

Immutability Alert!

Remember, tuples are immutable, so if you try to modify them, Python will throw a TypeError.

```
# This will cause a TypeError
my_tuple[0] = 'one'
```

When to Use Lists vs. Tuples

- **Lists**: When you need an ordered collection of items that you might need to modify, lists are your go-to.
- **Tuples**: When you need an ordered collection of items that should not be changed, opt for tuples.

Safety and Error Handling

Watch out for these common pitfalls:
1. **IndexError**: Happens when you try to access an index that doesn't exist in the list or tuple.
2. **TypeError**: Occurs when you attempt to modify a tuple.

Practical Exercises

1. **Exercise 1**: Create a list of your favorite fruits. Add two more fruits to it, and then remove the last fruit. Print the final list.
2. **Exercise 2**: Create a tuple of numbers from 1 to 5. Try modifying the second element. What error do you get?

Solutions to the Exercises

Solution to Exercise 1:

Here's how you could create a list of your favorite fruits, add two more fruits to it, remove the last fruit, and then print the final list.

```python
# Create a list of favorite fruits
favorite_fruits = ['apple', 'banana', 'cherry']

# Add two more fruits
favorite_fruits.append('grapes')
favorite_fruits.append('orange')

# Remove the last fruit
favorite_fruits.pop()

# Print the final list
print(favorite_fruits)   # Output: ['apple', 'banana', 'cherry', 'grapes']
```

Solution to Exercise 2:

To create a tuple of numbers from 1 to 5 and try modifying the second element, you would write the following code. You'll encounter a `TypeError` because tuples are immutable.

```python
# Create a tuple of numbers from 1 to 5
numbers = (1, 2, 3, 4, 5)

# Try modifying the second element
try:
    numbers[1] = 6
except TypeError as e:
    print(f"An error occurred: {e}")   # Output: An error occurred: 'tuple' object does
not support item assignment
```

Now you have the answers to the exercises, and hopefully, they help clarify the use and limitations of lists and tuples! Keep these solutions in mind as you continue your Python journey. They'll provide a good foundation for understanding more complex data structures later on.

Dictionaries and Sets

We've just cracked the surface with lists and tuples. Now, let's dive deeper into Python's treasure trove of data structures—specifically, dictionaries and sets. These might seem intimidating at first, but don't worry, we'll break them down piece by piece.

Learning Objectives:
- Understand what dictionaries and sets are
- Learn how to create and manipulate dictionaries and sets
- Know when to use dictionaries and sets in your code

What Are Dictionaries?

In Python, dictionaries are used to store key-value pairs. Think of them like a real-world dictionary. You look up a word (the key), and you get a definition (the value).

Creating a Dictionary

Creating a dictionary is straightforward. You can define an empty dictionary or initialize it with key-value pairs. Here's how:

```python
# Empty dictionary
my_empty_dict = {}

# Dictionary with key-value pairs
person = {"name": "John", "age": 30, "email": "john.doe@email.com"}
```

Accessing Values

To access the value associated with a particular key:

```python
print(person['name'])   # Output: "John"
```

Updating Values

You can update a dictionary by simply assigning a new value to an existing key:

```python
person['age'] = 31
```

Removing Key-Value Pairs

To remove a key-value pair, you can use the del statement:

```python
del person['email']
```

Common Pitfalls and Warnings

Be careful when accessing keys that don't exist; Python will throw a KeyError. To avoid this, use the get() method which returns None if the key doesn't exist.

```python
print(person.get('email'))   # Output: None
```

What Are Sets?

Sets are like lists but with a twist: they don't allow duplicate values. They're great for when you want to keep track of unique elements.

Creating a Set

To create a set, you can use the set() constructor or enclose your elements in curly braces {}.

```
# Empty set
my_empty_set = set()

# Set with elements
my_set = {1, 2, 3, 4}
```

Adding Elements
You can add elements to a set using the `add()` method:

```
my_set.add(5)    # {1, 2, 3, 4, 5}
```

Removing Elements
To remove an element, use the `remove()` method. Be cautious though; trying to remove an element that doesn't exist will raise a `KeyError`.

```
my_set.remove(1)    # {2, 3, 4, 5}
```

To avoid this error, you can use the `discard()` method, which does nothing if the element is not found.

Common Pitfalls and Warnings
Remember, sets are unordered. So, don't expect to retrieve elements in the same order you added them.

Practical Exercises:
Exercise   1:
Create a dictionary that holds information about a book like the title, author, and the year it was published. Then, update the year to the current year.
Exercise   2:
Create a set containing your five favorite movies. Then try adding a duplicate movie and observe what happens.

Solutions to the Exercises

Exercise 1:
Task:
Create a dictionary that holds information about a book like the title, author, and the year it was published. Then, update the year to the current year.
Solution:
Step 1: Create a dictionary with book information

```
book_info = {
    "title": "To Kill a Mockingbird",
```

```
        "author": "Harper Lee",
        "year_published": 1960
}
```

Step 2: Update the year to the current year

```
book_info['year_published'] = 2023
```

Step 3: Print the updated dictionary to confirm

```
print(book_info)
# Output: {'title': 'To Kill a Mockingbird', 'author': 'Harper Lee', 'year_published':
2023}
```

Exercise 2:
  Task:
Create a set containing your five favorite movies. Then try adding a duplicate movie and observe what happens.
  Solution:
Step 1: Create a set with your favorite movies

```
favorite_movies = {"The Shawshank Redemption", "Forrest Gump", "Inception", "The Dark
Knight", "Fight Club"}
```

Step 2: Add a duplicate movie

```
favorite_movies.add("Inception")
```

Step 3: Print the set to observe

```
print(favorite_movies)
# Output: {'Fight Club', 'Inception', 'The Dark Knight', 'Forrest Gump', 'The Shawshank
Redemption'}
```

Observation: You'll notice that adding a duplicate entry ("Inception" in this case) didn't change the set. That's because sets don't allow duplicate values, keeping only one instance of each element.
  And there you have it—Solutions to the Exercises that help you get hands-on experience with dictionaries and sets! Remember, practice makes perfect. So, keep coding!

Structuring Data with Nested Collections
  So, you've had your fill of lists, tuples, dictionaries, and sets. You're probably thinking, "What's next?" How about we start nesting these collections within one another? It's like Russian dolls but in code form! This approach allows us to create more complex and organized data structures, which can be a game-changer in many programming scenarios. Buckle up, because it's about to get nested!

36

Learning Objectives:
- Understand what nested collections are and why they're useful.
- Learn how to create and manipulate nested lists, tuples, dictionaries, and sets.
- Practice structuring data in multiple dimensions.

What Are Nested Collections?
Nested collections are essentially collections within collections—lists inside lists, dictionaries inside dictionaries, or any mix of these. They allow for more nuanced data organization, which is particularly helpful when dealing with complex information that has multiple layers or categories.

Why Use Nested Collections?
Think about a company's organizational chart. You have departments, and within those departments, you have teams. Within those teams, you have individual employees. A single list or dictionary won't cut it here. That's when nested collections come into play.

Nested Lists

How to Create a Nested List:
Step 1:
You can create a nested list just like you would create a regular list, but with an extra pair of square brackets.

```
# A list of three lists, each containing three numbers
nested_list = [[1, 2, 3], [4, 5, 6], [7, 8, 9]]
```

How to Access Elements:
Step 2:
Accessing elements in a nested list requires two indices: one for the inner list and one for the element within that inner list.

```
# Access the first list's first element
print(nested_list[0][0])   # Output: 1
```

Nested Dictionaries:

How to Create a Nested Dictionary:
Step 3:
Creating a nested dictionary is a bit more involved. Here's an example.

```
# Dictionary containing another dictionary
nested_dict = {
    "department": {
        "HR": ["Jim", "Pam"],
```

```
       "Engineering": ["Angela", "Dwight"]
   }
}
```

How to Access Elements:
Step 4:
Accessing elements in a nested dictionary involves chaining keys together.

```
# Access employees in the HR department
print(nested_dict["department"]["HR"])   # Output: ["Jim", "Pam"]
```

Safety and Error Handling:
Be cautious when working with nested collections. It's easy to lose track of brackets or keys, which can lead to errors. Always double-check your indices and keys.

Practical Exercises:
1. Create a nested list that represents a tic-tac-toe board. Make sure to initialize it with empty strings.

2. Create a nested dictionary that holds a student's grades for multiple subjects, each with different grading components (assignments, exams, etc.).

Absolutely, let's dive into the solutions to those practical exercises.

Solution to the Exercises

Solution to Exercise 1: Create a Nested List for Tic-Tac-Toe Board
For a tic-tac-toe board, you'd typically have a 3x3 grid, which you can represent with a nested list of 3 lists, each containing 3 empty strings.
Here's how you can do it:

```
# Initialize an empty tic-tac-toe board
tic_tac_toe_board = [["", "", ""], ["", "", ""], ["", "", ""]]

# To visualize, the board will look like this:
# [["", "", ""]
#  ["", "", ""]
#  ["", "", ""]]
```

Solution to Exercise 2: Nested Dictionary for Student's Grades
Suppose we want to create a nested dictionary for a student named "John" that includes grades for multiple subjects—Math, Science, and English. Each subject has grades for assignments and exams.

Here's how you could structure this data:

```python
# Nested dictionary for student grades
student_grades = {
    "John": {
        "Math": {
            "Assignments": [90, 85, 77],
            "Exams": [88, 76]
        },
        "Science": {
            "Assignments": [92, 89],
            "Exams": [84, 77]
        },
        "English": {
            "Assignments": [85, 82, 94],
            "Exams": [90]
        }
    }
}

# To fetch John's Math exam grades
print(student_grades["John"]["Math"]["Exams"])   # Output: [88, 76]
```

You could then easily expand this structure to include more students, subjects, or grading components.
There you have it! Solutions to the exercises that should help you get a good grasp of working with nested collections. Keep practicing, and you'll get the hang of it in no time!

Chapter 5: Advanced Data Structures Concepts

_ Lists

List Concatenation

Joining two lists together in Python is simple and straightforward. You can concatenate two lists by using the + operator.

Example:

```
list1 = [1, 2, 3]
list2 = [4, 5, 6]
concatenated_list = list1 + list2
print(concatenated_list)  # Output: [1, 2, 3, 4, 5, 6]
```

Repetition Operator

If you want to repeat the elements of a list a certain number of times, use the * operator.

Example:

```
my_list = [1, 2, 3]
repeated_list = my_list * 3
print(repeated_list)  # Output: [1, 2, 3, 1, 2, 3, 1, 2, 3]
```

Comparing Lists

In Python, you can compare lists using comparison operators like ==, !=, <, >, <=, and >=.

Example:

```
list1 = [1, 2, 3]
list2 = [1, 2, 3]
list3 = [4, 5, 6]

print(list1 == list2)  # Output: True
print(list1 == list3)  # Output: False
```

List Comprehensions

List comprehensions provide a concise way to create lists. The general syntax is [expression for element in iterable if condition].

Example:

```
squares = [x*x for x in range(5)]
print(squares)  # Output: [0, 1, 4, 9, 16]
```

List Methods

append() method
The `append()` method adds a single element to the end of the list.

```python
my_list = [1, 2, 3]
my_list.append(4)
print(my_list)   # Output: [1, 2, 3, 4]
```

insert() method
The `insert()` method adds a single element at a specific index.

```python
my_list = [1, 3]
my_list.insert(1, 2)
print(my_list)   # Output: [1, 2, 3]
(Continued in the next reply due to character limits)
```

index() method
The `index()` method returns the index of the first occurrence of an element in a list.

```python
my_list = [1, 2, 3, 4, 5]
index_of_four = my_list.index(4)
print(index_of_four)   # Output: 3
```

remove() method
The `remove()` method removes the first occurrence of an element from the list.

```python
my_list = [1, 2, 3, 4, 5]
my_list.remove(3)
print(my_list)   # Output: [1, 2, 4, 5]
```

count() method
The `count()` method counts the number of occurrences of an element in a list.

```python
my_list = [1, 2, 2, 3, 4, 4, 4, 5]
count_of_four = my_list.count(4)
print(count_of_four)   # Output: 3
```

clear() method
The `clear()` method removes all elements from the list.

```python
my_list = [1, 2, 3]
my_list.clear()
print(my_list)   # Output: []
```

sort() method

The `sort()` method sorts the elements of a list.

```
my_list = [3, 1, 4, 1, 5, 9, 2, 6, 5]
my_list.sort()
print(my_list)  # Output: [1, 1, 2, 3, 4, 5, 5, 6, 9]
```

reverse() method

The `reverse()` method reverses the elements of the list.

```
my_list = [1, 2, 3]
my_list.reverse()
print(my_list)  # Output: [3, 2, 1]
```

extends() method

The `extend()` method adds all elements from another list or iterable.

```
my_list = [1, 2, 3]
additional_elements = [4, 5, 6]
my_list.extend(additional_elements)
print(my_list)  # Output: [1, 2, 3, 4, 5, 6]
```

pop() method

The `pop()` method removes and returns an element from a specified position in the list. If no index is provided, it removes and returns the last element.

```
my_list = [1, 2, 3, 4]
popped_element = my_list.pop(2)
print(popped_element)  # Output: 3
print(my_list)  # Output: [1, 2, 4]
```

Certainly, let's continue diving into the nitty-gritty of dictionaries, sets, and their methods.

_ *Dictionaries*

Getting Length of Dictionary using len()

To get the number of key-value pairs in a dictionary, use the `len()` function.

```
my_dict = {'name': 'Alice', 'age': 30}
print(len(my_dict))  # Output: 2
```

Iterating through elements using for loop

You can loop through a dictionary by keys, values, or both.

```
# By keys
for key in my_dict.keys():
```

```
    print(key)

# By values
for value in my_dict.values():
    print(value)


# By key-value pairs
for key, value in my_dict.items():
    print(f"{key}: {value}")
```

Membership Operators with Dictionary

You can check for the presence of a key using in and not in.

```
# Check for key
print('name' in my_dict)   # Output: True
```

Comparison Operators with Dictionary

Python dictionaries cannot be compared using standard comparison operators like <, >, etc. You have to loop through and compare manually.

Dictionary Methods

keys() method
Returns a list of all keys.

```
keys = my_dict.keys()
```

values() method
Returns a list of all values.

```
values = my_dict.values()
```

items() method
Returns a list of key-value tuples.

```
items = my_dict.items()
```

get() method
Returns the value for the given key, if exists, else None.

```
value = my_dict.get('name', 'Unknown')
```

pop() method
Removes a key-value pair and returns the value.

```
age = my_dict.pop('age')
```

popitem() method
Removes and returns the last key-value pair.

```
item = my_dict.popitem()
```

copy() method
Returns a shallow copy of the dictionary.

```
new_dict = my_dict.copy()
```

clear() method
Removes all elements from the dictionary.

```
my_dict.clear()
```

Sure, let's continue by exploring Sets!

_ *Sets*

Looping through sets
Looping through a set is straightforward. Just remember, sets are unordered collections.

```
my_set = {1, 2, 3}
for item in my_set:
    print(item)
```

Membership Operator in and not in
You can check for the existence of an item using the in and not in operators.

```
print(1 in my_set)   # Output: True
print(4 not in my_set)   # Output: True
```

Subset and Supersets
Use issubset() and issuperset() methods to check subsets and supersets.

```
another_set = {1, 2}
print(another_set.issubset(my_set))   # Output: True
print(my_set.issuperset(another_set))   # Output: True
```

Comparing Sets
You can use == or != to compare sets. Sets are equal if they contain the same elements, regardless of the order.

```
print({1, 2, 3} == {3, 2, 1})   # Output: True
```

Union and Intersection of Sets

The `union()` method returns a new set with all distinct elements from both sets, while `intersection()` returns common elements.

```
print(my_set.union(another_set))   # Output: {1, 2, 3}
print(my_set.intersection(another_set))   # Output: {1, 2}
```

Difference and Symmetric Difference of Sets

The `difference()` method returns a set containing elements present in the first set but not in the second. `symmetric_difference()` returns a set containing elements that are in either of the sets but not in both.

```
print(my_set.difference(another_set))   # Output: {3}
print(my_set.symmetric_difference(another_set))   # Output: {3}
```

And there you have it—a deep dive into lists, dictionaries, and sets in Python. Remember, each data structure has its unique features, pros, and cons, so choose wisely based on your specific needs.

Certainly! Here's an in-depth look at Tuples in Python.

_ *Tuples*

Accessing Elements

You can access elements in a tuple using indexing, just like you would with a list.

```
my_tuple = (1, 2, 3)
print(my_tuple[0])   # Output: 1
```

Slicing Tuples

Slice a tuple using the `:` operator.

```
print(my_tuple[1:3])   # Output: (2, 3)
```

Concatenating Tuples

You can concatenate two tuples using the + operator.

```
new_tuple = my_tuple + (4, 5)
print(new_tuple)   # Output: (1, 2, 3, 4, 5)
```

Nested Tuples

Tuples can contain other tuples as elements, making it easy to create complex data structures.

```
nested_tuple = (1, (2, 3), 4)
print(nested_tuple[1][0])   # Output: 2
```

Immutability

Remember that tuples are immutable. This means that once a tuple is created, its content can't be changed.

```
# This will raise a TypeError
# my_tuple[1] = 2
```

Tuple Methods

Tuples don't offer as many built-in methods as lists, but you can still use `index()` to find the index of an element and `count()` to find the number of occurrences of a particular element.

```
print(my_tuple.index(2))   # Output: 1
print(my_tuple.count(1))   # Output: 1
```

Tuple Unpacking

You can unpack a tuple by assigning its values to multiple variables.

```
a, b, c = my_tuple
print(a, b, c)   # Output: 1 2 3
```

Additional Tuple Methods and Operations

Length of Tuple

You can find the length of a tuple using the `len()` function, similar to lists and dictionaries.

```
print(len(my_tuple))   # Output: 3
```

Membership Operator: `in` and `not in`

You can check for the existence of an element within a tuple using the `in` and `not in` membership operators.

```
print(2 in my_tuple)       # Output: True
print(5 not in my_tuple)   # Output: True
```

Min and Max Elements

Find the minimum and maximum elements in a tuple using the `min()` and `max()` functions, respectively.

```
print(min(my_tuple))   # Output: 1
print(max(my_tuple))   # Output: 3
```

Converting Lists to Tuples and Vice Versa

You can convert a list to a tuple using the `tuple()` constructor, and a tuple to a list using the `list()` constructor.

```
my_list = [1, 2, 3]
converted_tuple = tuple(my_list)

print(converted_tuple)   # Output: (1, 2, 3)

# Converting back to list
converted_list = list(converted_tuple)
print(converted_list)   # Output: [1, 2, 3]
```

Tuple Repetition

You can repeat the elements in a tuple a specified number of times using the `*` operator.

```
repeated_tuple = my_tuple * 2
print(repeated_tuple)   # Output: (1, 2, 3, 1, 2, 3)
```

Exercises

Exercise 1: Dictionary Manipulation

Create a dictionary with 5 key-value pairs. Add a new pair, update an existing pair, and delete a pair.

Exercise 2: Set Operations

Create two sets and perform union, intersection, difference, and symmetric difference operations.

Exercise 3: Tuple Creation and Concatenation

Create two tuples and concatenate them. Then, find the index of an element.

Solutions to the Exercises

Solution to Exercise 1:

```
# Create a dictionary
my_dict = {'name': 'Alice', 'age': 30, 'gender': 'F', 'country': 'USA', 'language':
'English'}

# Add a new pair
```

```
my_dict['profession'] = 'Engineer'

# Update an existing pair
my_dict['age'] = 31

# Delete a pair
del my_dict['language']


print(my_dict)
```

Solution to Exercise 2:

```
# Create two sets
set1 = {1, 2, 3, 4, 5}
set2 = {4, 5, 6, 7, 8}

# Union
print("Union:", set1.union(set2))

# Intersection
print("Intersection:", set1.intersection(set2))

# Difference
print("Difference:", set1.difference(set2))

# Symmetric Difference
print("Symmetric Difference:", set1.symmetric_difference(set2))
```

That wraps up this chapter on advanced data structures! Stay tuned for more Python goodness!

Solution to Exercise 3:

```
# Create two tuples
tuple1 = (1, 2, 3)
tuple2 = (4, 5, 6)

# Concatenate them
concatenated_tuple = tuple1 + tuple2
print("Concatenated Tuple:", concatenated_tuple)

# Find index of an element
index = concatenated_tuple.index(4)
print("Index of 4:", index)
```

try also this

```
# Create a nested tuple
nested_tuple = (1, (2, 3), 4)

# Access the inner tuple
inner_tuple = nested_tuple[1]
print("Inner Tuple:", inner_tuple)
```

Chapter 6: Control Structures and Loops

Intro to Structures and Loops

Welcome to the world of control structures and loops in Python! If data types and variables are the nouns of Python, consider control structures and loops as the verbs. They're the action heroes, making things happen.

What Are Control Structures?

In a nutshell, control structures direct the flow of your program. Imagine you're the director of a movie; you don't want all the scenes to play out randomly, right? Instead, you'd prefer to control the sequence of scenes based on the script. The same goes for programming. Control structures enable you to execute particular blocks of code only under certain conditions or repeatedly. Python provides several types of control structures including conditional statements (`if`, `elif`, `else`) and loops (`for`, `while`).

Why Are They Important?

Control structures are the backbone of any programming language. They give your programs the capability to make decisions (`if it's raining, carry an umbrella`) and to perform tasks repeatedly (`for each item in this list, do something`). Hence, they're pretty darn crucial.

The Three C's of Control Structures

1. **Choice**: Making decisions with `if`, `else`, and `elif`.
2. **Cycle**: Looping with `for` and `while`.
3. **Control**: Managing loop execution with `break`, `continue`, and `pass`.

Conditional Statements

Think of conditional statements as a series of "if this, then that" scenarios. The `if` statement checks a condition: if it's `True`, then the block of code under it will execute. You can add as many `elif` (else if) conditions as you want after that. Lastly, the `else` will catch anything that didn't meet the previous conditions.

Here's a brief example to explain `if`, `elif`, and `else`:

```
x = 10
if x > 5:
    print("x is greater than 5")
elif x == 5:
    print("x is equal to 5")
else:
    print("x is less than 5")
```

Loops

Loops are the workhorses of any program. You've got two types to play with:

1. **For Loops**: These loops iterate over a sequence (lists, tuples, dictionaries, etc.) and execute a block of code.

```
for i in range(5):
    print(i)   # Output: 0, 1, 2, 3, 4
```

2. **While Loops**: These loops keep executing as long as a specified condition is met.

```
count = 0
while count < 5:
    print(count)   # Output: 0, 1, 2, 3, 4
    count += 1
```

Controlling Loop Execution

Sometimes you'll want to exit a loop early if a condition is met (break), skip an iteration (continue), or do absolutely nothing (pass).

```
for i in range(5):
    if i == 3:
        break   # Exits the loop, so output will be 0, 1, 2
    print(i)
```

Safety First!

Watch out for infinite loops! In a while loop, if the condition never turns False, your loop will run indefinitely, and nobody wants that. Always double-check your exit conditions.

Practical Exercises:

1. **Create Your Own Conditional**: Use if, elif, and else to check the grades of a student and print whether they are passing, failing, or excelling.
2. **Summing Up Numbers**: Use a for loop to calculate the sum of numbers from 1 to 100.
3. **Guess the Number**: Implement a while loop where the user has to guess a pre-defined number.

Solutions to the Exercises

Exercise 1: Create Your Own Conditional

In this exercise, you were asked to use if, elif, and else statements to check the grades of a student and print whether they are passing, failing, or excelling. Here's one way to do it:

```
# Input: Student's grade
grade = int(input("Enter the student's grade: "))
```

```
# Conditional checks
if grade >= 90:
    print("The student is excelling!")
elif grade >= 70:
    print("The student is passing.")
else:
    print("The student is failing.")
```

Exercise 2: Summing Up Numbers

You were tasked with using a `for` loop to calculate the sum of numbers from 1 to 100. Here it is:

```
# Initialize sum to 0
total_sum = 0

# Loop through numbers 1 to 100
for i in range(1, 101):
    total_sum += i   # Add each number to total_sum

print("The sum of numbers from 1 to 100 is:", total_sum)
```

Exercise 3: Guess the Number

The goal was to implement a `while` loop where the user has to guess a pre-defined number. Here's a sample solution:

```
# Pre-defined number to guess
target_number = 23

# Initialize user's guess to None
user_guess = None

while user_guess != target_number:
    # Get user's guess
    user_guess = int(input("Guess the number: "))

    if user_guess < target_number:
        print("Too low! Try again.")
    elif user_guess > target_number:
        print("Too high! Try again.")
    else:
        print("Congratulations! You've guessed the correct number.")
```

These are just sample solutions. Feel free to get creative and maybe add some additional features, like giving the user hints or limiting the number of guesses in Exercise 3. Happy coding!

Conditionals: if, else, and elif Statements

Alright, folks! We've got a juicy topic here: Conditionals. Conditionals are the bread and butter of any programming language, and Python is no exception. They are your go-to tool for making decisions in your code. You'll be using `if`, `else`, and `elif` statements to tell your computer what to do under different conditions. So, let's dive right in!

What is a Conditional Statement?

In plain English, a conditional statement is a set of rules you define for your program to follow based on certain conditions. Imagine you're an air traffic controller. You wouldn't tell a plane to land if the runway isn't clear, right? You'd give different instructions based on different situations. That's what conditional statements in Python do—they control the "air traffic" of your program's logic.

The `if` Statement

The `if` statement is the simplest form of a conditional. It checks if something is true and then executes a block of code if that condition is met. Here's the syntax:

```
if some_condition:
    # Do something
```
For example:

```
if 3 > 2:
    print("3 is greater than 2.")
```

The `else` Statement

Sometimes, you want to do something when your `if` condition isn't met. That's when `else` comes in.

```
if some_condition:
    # Do something
else:
    # Do something else
```

The `elif` Statement

`elif` stands for "else if." It allows you to add extra conditions to your `if` statement. Here's how you can use `elif`:

```
if some_condition:
    # Do something
elif another_condition:
    # Do something else
```

```
else:
    # Do yet something else
```

Nested Conditionals

You can even nest `if` statements within other `if` statements, but watch out for complexity.

```
if condition1:
    if condition2:
        # Do something
```

A Real-World Example

Let's say we want to write a Python program to determine if a student has passed or failed an exam.

```
# Input: Student's grade
grade = int(input("Enter your grade: "))

# Conditional checks
if grade >= 70:
    print("You passed!")
else:
    print("You failed.")
```

Practical Exercises

Exercise 1: User Age Group

Write a Python program that takes the age of a user as input and categorizes them into one of three age groups: "Child," "Adult," or "Senior."

Exercise 2: Simple Calculator

Create a simple calculator that takes two numbers and an operator (+, -, *, /) as input and performs the corresponding calculation.

Exercise 3: Nested Conditionals

Write a Python program that first asks the user if they're a vegetarian. If yes, ask if they eat eggs. Display appropriate meal choices based on their answers.

There you go! We've covered the basics of `if`, `else`, and `elif` statements. I can't stress enough how important these are for control flow in your Python programs. Stay tuned for our next section where we'll explore loops!

Keep in mind that improper use of conditionals can lead to errors or bugs in your code. So practice caution and always double-check your logic.

Solutions to the Exercises

Solution to Exercise 1: User Age Group

Here's a Python script that categorizes the user's age into one of three age groups: "Child," "Adult," or "Senior."

```python
# Take the user's age as input
age = int(input("Enter your age: "))


# Determine the age group
if age < 18:
    print("You are a Child.")
elif age >= 18 and age < 65:
    print("You are an Adult.")
else:
    print("You are a Senior.")
```

Solution to Exercise 2: Simple Calculator

This Python program takes two numbers and an operator as input and performs the corresponding calculation. Check it out:

```python
# Take user input
num1 = float(input("Enter the first number: "))
num2 = float(input("Enter the second number: "))
operator = input("Enter an operator (+, -, *, /): ")

# Perform the calculation
if operator == "+":
    print(f"The result is: {num1 + num2}")
elif operator == "-":
    print(f"The result is: {num1 - num2}")
elif operator == "*":
    print(f"The result is: {num1 * num2}")
elif operator == "/":
    if num2 != 0:
        print(f"The result is: {num1 / num2}")
    else:
        print("Cannot divide by zero.")
else:
    print("Invalid operator.")
```

Solution to Exercise 3: Nested Conditionals

This Python program asks the user if they're a vegetarian and if they eat eggs, then displays appropriate meal choices. Here's the solution:

```python
# Ask user about vegetarianism
is_vegetarian = input("Are you a vegetarian? (yes/no): ").lower()

# Nested conditionals for meal choices
if is_vegetarian == 'yes':
    eats_eggs = input("Do you eat eggs? (yes/no): ").lower()
    if eats_eggs == 'yes':
        print("You can have a veggie omelette.")
    else:
        print("You can have a veggie stir-fry.")
else:
    print("You can have a steak.")
```

Loops: for and while loops

Let's dive into the world of loops in Python. Loops are the bread and butter of programming, and Python provides two primary types: the `for` loop and the `while` loop. Let's start by digging into each.

The For Loop

A `for` loop is perfect when you know how many times you want to iterate. This loop cycles through a sequence (like a list, tuple, or string), executing a block of code for each item in the sequence.

```python
# A simple for loop example
for i in range(5):
    print(i)
```

This prints the numbers 0 through 4. Here `range(5)` returns a sequence from 0 to 4, and the `for` loop iterates through this sequence.

Nested For Loop: You can also have a `for` loop inside another `for` loop, known as nested loops.

```python
# Nested for loop to print a 2D array
for i in range(3):
    for j in range(3):
        print(i, j)
```

Be cautious with nested loops; they can eat up computing time if not carefully managed.

56

The While Loop

While `for` loops are used when you know the number of iterations, `while` loops are used when the number of iterations is unknown.

```python
# A simple while loop example
i = 0
while i < 5:
    print(i)
    i += 1
```

Here, the `while` loop continues as long as the condition `i < 5` is True.

Infinite While Loop: Be cautious; a `while` loop can become an infinite loop if the condition never becomes False. Always ensure there's a way out of the loop.

```python
# This is an infinite loop. DO NOT run this!
while True:
    pass
```

For vs. While: When to Use Which?

Use `for` loops when you know the number of iterations, usually when you're cycling through a sequence like a list or string. Use `while` loops when the number of iterations is unknown or dependent on a specific condition.

Exercises

1. Write a `for` loop to sum all the even numbers from 1 to 100.
2. Create a `while` loop to find the smallest power of 2 that's larger than 1000.
3. Implement a nested `for` loop to print the multiplication table from 1 to 10.

So, there you go! That's the crux of loops in Python. Whether it's running the same block of code for each element in a list or performing a specific task while a condition is met, loops are the go-to constructs. Now, onto the exercises to put your newfound knowledge to the test!

Solution to the exercises

Exercise 1: Sum All Even Numbers from 1 to 100

To sum all the even numbers from 1 to 100, you can use a `for` loop.

```python
sum_even = 0
for i in range(2, 101, 2):
    sum_even += i
print("The sum of all even numbers from 1 to 100 is:", sum_even)
```

Here, `range(2, 101, 2)` starts from 2 and goes up to 100, incrementing by 2 each time. This ensures that you only consider even numbers.

Exercise 2: Smallest Power of 2 Larger than 1000

A `while` loop is perfect for this task because you don't know how many iterations you'll need.

```
power_of_two = 1
while power_of_two <= 1000:
    power_of_two *= 2
print("The smallest power of 2 larger than 1000 is:", power_of_two)
```

This loop will keep doubling `power_of_two` until it becomes greater than 1000.

Exercise 3: Multiplication Table from 1 to 10

A nested `for` loop will work well for this task.

```
for i in range(1, 11):
    for j in range(1, 11):
        print(i * j, end="\t")
    print()  # New line after each row
```

Here, the inner loop iterates for each value of the outer loop, and we print the product of `i` and `j`. The `end="\t"` ensures that the numbers are separated by tabs.

I hope these solutions help you better understand loops in Python! Feel free to give them a try and play around with the code.

Controlling Loop Execution: break, continue, and pass

Hey, good to see you're progressing! We've talked about loops and how useful they can be, but sometimes you need a little more control over them. That's where `break`, `continue`, and `pass` come in. These are special keywords in Python that give you that extra layer of control you might need when your code is doing something repetitive. So, let's take a closer look at each.

The `break` Statement

First up is `break`. This keyword will exit the loop it's in, straight away. No questions asked, no turning back. This is super handy if you need to stop a loop when a certain condition is met.

Example:

```
for i in range(10):
    print(i)
    if i == 5:
        break
```

In this example, the loop will only run until `i` equals 5, then it's game over.

58

The `continue` Statement

Next, let's chat about `continue`. This keyword is like the polite version of `break`. Instead of ending the loop, it just skips to the next iteration, leaving the rest of the loop untouched.

Example:

```python
for i in range(10):
    if i % 2 == 0:
        continue
    print(i)
```

Here, only the odd numbers get printed, skipping all even numbers because of the `continue` statement.

The `pass` Statement

Finally, let's talk about `pass`. This is Python's way of saying "move along, nothing to see here." Seriously, it does absolutely nothing and is usually used as a placeholder.

Example:

```python
for i in range(10):
    if i == 5:
        pass
    print(i)
```

The loop will run as if the `pass` statement wasn't even there. It's often used when you're drafting out structures but aren't sure what to put in them yet.

Mixing Them Up

You can even use these statements together for more complex control.

Example:

```python
for i in range(10):
    if i == 5:
        break
    elif i % 2 == 0:
        continue
    else:
        pass
    print(i)
```

Exercises

1. **Break Exercise**: Write a loop that adds numbers from 1 to 100 but stops when the sum reaches over 500.
2. **Continue Exercise**: Write a loop that prints all numbers from 1 to 20 but skips any number that is divisible by 3.

3. **Pass Exercise**: Create a loop that counts from 1 to 10. Use the `pass` statement for numbers between 4 and 7, but print the rest.

Key Takeaways
- `break` ends the loop immediately.
- `continue` skips to the next iteration.
- `pass` does absolutely nothing.

Alright, that's your comprehensive dive into controlling loop execution. Have fun playing around with these, but remember: with great power comes great responsibility. Use them wisely! Next up, we'll practice what you've learned.

Solution to the Exercises

Break Exercise
Write a loop that adds numbers from 1 to 100 but stops when the sum reaches over 500.
Solution:
```
total_sum = 0
for i in range(1, 101):
    total_sum += i
    if total_sum > 500:
        print(f"The sum reached {total_sum} at i = {i}. Breaking the loop.")
        break
```
In this loop, we start summing numbers from 1 to 100. The moment the `total_sum` exceeds 500, we use the `break` statement to exit the loop.

Continue Exercise
Write a loop that prints all numbers from 1 to 20 but skips any number that is divisible by 3.
Solution:
```
for i in range(1, 21):
    if i % 3 == 0:
        continue
    print(i)
```
Here, we iterate numbers from 1 to 20. If a number is divisible by 3, we skip printing it and move to the next iteration using `continue`.

Pass Exercise
Create a loop that counts from 1 to 10. Use the `pass` statement for numbers between 4 and 7, but print the rest.
Solution:

```
for i in range(1, 11):
    if 4 <= i <= 7:
        pass
    else:
        print(i)
```

In this example, the numbers from 4 to 7 will hit the `pass` statement, essentially doing nothing. All other numbers get printed.

There you have it! The solutions to the exercises that allow you to practice controlling your loops. I hope these helped cement your understanding of when and how to use `break`, `continue`, and `pass`. Feel free to run these examples and tweak them to get a feel for how they behave. On to the next section!

Chapter 7: Looping through Data Structures

When you're dealing with data structures like lists, tuples, dictionaries, and sets, it's often necessary to loop through them to perform some action on each element. Understanding how to effectively loop through these structures is essential for coding efficiency. Let's dive into it.

_ *Looping through Lists*

Lists are perhaps the most straightforward data structure to loop through. The commonly used `for` loop works wonderfully with lists.

```
my_list = [1, 2, 3, 4, 5]
for item in my_list:
    print(item)
```

Exercise 1: Create a list of fruits and use a for loop to print each fruit capitalized.

_ *Looping through Tuples*

Tuples are quite similar to lists in terms of looping. You can use a `for` loop to iterate through each element of the tuple.

```
my_tuple = (1, 2, 3, 4, 5)
for item in my_tuple:
    print(item)
```

Exercise 2: Create a tuple containing different types of vegetables. Loop through it and print each vegetable in upper case.

_ *Looping through Dictionaries*

Dictionaries are unique because they store key-value pairs. You can loop through dictionaries by their keys, values, or key-value pairs.

- Looping through keys:

```
my_dict = {'apple': 1, 'banana': 2, 'cherry': 3}
for key in my_dict:
    print(key)
```

- Looping through values:

```
for value in my_dict.values():
    print(value)
```

- Looping through key-value pairs:

```
for key, value in my_dict.items():
    print(f"The key is {key} and the value is {value}")
```

Exercise 3: Create a dictionary with country names as keys and their capitals as values. Loop through it and print each key-value pair in a formatted sentence.

Looping through Sets

Sets are collections of unique elements. Looping through sets is similar to looping through lists or tuples, but remember that sets are unordered.

```
my_set = {1, 2, 3, 4, 5}
for item in my_set:
    print(item)
```

Exercise 4: Create a set of numbers. Loop through the set and print each number multiplied by 2.

Exercises Solutions

1. Looping through a list of fruits and printing each fruit capitalized:

```
fruits = ['apple', 'banana', 'cherry']
for fruit in fruits:
    print(fruit.upper())
```

2. Looping through a tuple of vegetables and printing each vegetable in upper case:

```
vegetables = ('carrot', 'potato', 'spinach')
for vegetable in vegetables:
    print(vegetable.upper())
```

3. Looping through a dictionary and printing each key-value pair in a formatted sentence:

```
countries = {'USA': 'Washington, D.C.', 'France': 'Paris', 'Japan': 'Tokyo'}
for country, capital in countries.items():
    print(f"The capital of {country} is {capital}.")
```

4. Looping through a set of numbers and printing each number multiplied by 2:

```
numbers = {1, 2, 3, 4, 5}
for number in numbers:
    print(number * 2)
```

Looping through various data structures is a fundamental skill in Python programming. Whether you're working with lists, tuples, dictionaries, or sets, Python gives you the flexibility to loop through them in a way that makes your code efficient and clean.

Chapter 8: Functions and Modules

Intro to Functions and Modules

Welcome to one of the most transformative aspects of programming: functions and modules. Here, you're going to realize that you don't have to reinvent the wheel every time you code. You can reuse pieces of your code, call upon Python's extensive libraries, and keep your program tidy and efficient. So, what are functions and modules, and why should you care? Let's break it down.

What is a Function?

In the simplest terms, a function is a block of organized, reusable code that performs a specific task. Think of a function like a machine in a factory. You feed it some raw materials (inputs), it does something useful (processes the inputs), and then it gives you a finished product (the output).

For example, suppose you've written a piece of code that calculates the square root of a number and then rounds it to two decimal places. That's great, but what if you need to do this in multiple parts of your program? Instead of writing the same code over and over, you can wrap it up in a function and call that function whenever you need it.

The Anatomy of a Function

A function in Python typically has a name, parameters (optional), and a block of code. The format generally looks like this:

```
def function_name(parameters):
    # Your code here
    return output
```

Here, `def` indicates that you're defining a function, followed by the function name and parameters within parentheses. Finally, you write the function's code block indented under the `def` line. The optional `return` statement sends an output back to the part of the program that called the function.

Function Arguments and Return Values

A function can accept inputs, known as arguments, and return outputs. Arguments are variables that you pass into the function when you call it. These variables are placeholders that get replaced with actual values when the function is executed. The values that a function sends back to the calling program are known as return values.

Built-In Functions

Python comes packed with a treasure trove of built-in functions like `print()`, `len()`, `type()`, and many more. These are functions that are always available for you to use, and they perform basic operations.

Why Use Functions?

1. Reusability: Write once, use everywhere.

2. Modularity: Break down complex tasks into smaller, manageable pieces.

3. Simplifies Debugging: It's easier to debug smaller blocks of code than large monoliths.

4. Code Sharing: Share functions across multiple programs or even with other people.

What is a Module?

A module is essentially a file containing Python definitions, functions, and statements. You can put an assortment of function definitions in a module, which can then be imported into other Python scripts.

Why Use Modules?

1. Code Organization: Keep your program organized by breaking it into multiple files.

2. Code Reusability: Import the module in various Python scripts.

3. Namespace Management: Functions in a module won't interfere with variables or functions in other modules.

How to Import a Module?

Python makes importing a module incredibly straightforward. You simply use the `import` keyword followed by the module name.

```
import math
```

Once imported, you can use any function or variable defined in that module by prefixing it with the module name, like so:

```
result = math.sqrt(25)
```

Exercises

1. Write a function that reverses a string.
2. Create a function that takes two numbers as arguments and returns their sum.
3. Write a function that accepts a list of numbers and returns their average.

So, that's a wrap for our intro! Now, you should have a good understanding of what functions and modules are and why they are crucial in Python programming. Ready to take the leap and delve deeper? Let's go!

Remember, always code safely and efficiently by reusing and modularizing your code. Now, it's your turn to try your hand at the exercises!

Solutions to the exercises

Exercise 1: Reverse a String

Here's a Python function that reverses a string.

```
def reverse_string(s):
    return s[::-1]
```

```
# Test the function
print(reverse_string("Hello"))   # Output should be "olleH"
```

Exercise 2: Sum of Two Numbers

Here's how you can create a function that takes two numbers as arguments and returns their sum.

```
def sum_two_numbers(a, b):
    return a + b

# Test the function
print(sum_two_numbers(5, 10))   # Output should be 15
```

Exercise 3: Average of a List of Numbers

And finally, here's a function that accepts a list of numbers and returns their average.

```
def average(numbers):
    return sum(numbers) / len(numbers)

# Test the function
print(average([1, 2, 3, 4, 5]))   # Output should be 3.0
```

These are straightforward solutions to the exercises, designed to help you practice the basics of function creation and usage in Python. Notice how each function is reusable, so you can easily plug them into any part of your program where you might need these specific tasks performed.

Feel free to test these functions more comprehensively with different inputs to ensure they meet your requirements.

Creating and Utilizing Functions

In simple terms, a function is a block of reusable code that performs a specific task. Instead of rewriting the same lines of code multiple times, you can just call a function. How cool is that?

Here's an example of a simple function that prints "Hello, World!":

```
def greet_world():
    print("Hello, World!")
```

To use this function, all you need to do is call it like this:

```
greet_world()   # Outputs: Hello, World!
```

Anatomy of a Function

The `def` keyword starts the function definition, followed by the function name (`greet_world` in our case) and parentheses. The code inside the function is indented, and this block of code is what runs when the function is called.

```
def function_name(parameters):
    # Your code here
```

Parameters and Arguments

Notice the term "parameters" above? When defining a function, you can specify parameters, which are values you'll feed into the function later. When you actually use the function, the values you provide are called "arguments."

Here's a function that takes two numbers and returns their sum:

```
def add_numbers(a, b):
    return a + b
```

Return Statement

Ah, the `return` keyword. This allows your function to send some value back after it's done running. If you skip the return statement, Python will return `None`.

Using Functions in Real-life Scenarios

Let's say you're building a weather app. You could create a function that converts temperatures from Fahrenheit to Celsius.

```
def fahrenheit_to_celsius(fahrenheit):
    return (fahrenheit - 32) * 5/9
```

Local and Global Scope

Variables defined inside a function are in the "local scope," which means they can't be accessed outside the function. Variables defined outside any function are in the "global scope."

```
x = 10   # Global variable

def show_x():
    y = 5   # Local variable
    print(x)

show_x()   # Prints 10
```

Some Cautions
1. **Variable Scope**: Be cautious about where variables are defined. Local variables can't be accessed outside their function.

2. **Return Statements**: If you forget the `return` keyword, your function will return `None`, which could be confusing.

Exercises
1. **Write a function that calculates the area of a circle given its radius.**
3. **Develop a function that sorts a list of numbers in ascending order.**

Solutions to the Exercises
Certainly! Let's take a look at the solutions for each of the exercises.

Exercise 1: Calculate the Area of a Circle
To calculate the area of a circle given its radius, you can use the formula `Area = π * radius^2`.

```python
import math   # We need this for the value of pi


def circle_area(radius):
    return math.pi * (radius ** 2)
Test the function:


print(circle_area(5))    # Output: 78.53981633974483
print(circle_area(10))   # Output: 314.1592653589793
```

Exercise 2: Sort a List of Numbers
To sort a list of numbers in ascending order, you can use the `sorted()` built-in function or sort it manually.

```python
def sort_list(nums):
    return sorted(nums)
```

Or, doing it manually using a simple sorting algorithm like bubble sort:

```python
def sort_list(nums):
    n = len(nums)
    for i in range(n):
        for j in range(0, n-i-1):
            if nums[j] > nums[j+1]:
                nums[j], nums[j+1] = nums[j+1], nums[j]
    return nums
```

Test the function:

```
print(sort_list([34, 7, 23, 32, 5, 62]))   # Output: [5, 7, 23, 32, 34, 62]
print(sort_list([5, 2, 9, 1, 5, 6]))    # Output: [1, 2, 5, 5, 6, 9]
```

And there you go! You've successfully solved the exercises. Great work! Now, not only do you know how to create and use functions, but you've also got some practical experience under your belt. Keep it up!

Creating and Utilizing Modules

We've looked at variables, functions, and control structures, but now it's time to up the ante and look at how to organize our code better. Trust me, as your programs grow, you'll thank your stars you learned about modules.

What are Modules?

A module is basically a file containing Python code. It could have functions, classes, or variables that you'd like to use in other Python scripts. The key idea behind modules is code reusability. You write once and use it multiple times across different projects. So, it's like having a toolkit of handy utilities and functions that you can carry everywhere. Neat, huh?

How to Create a Module

Creating a module is as simple as pie. You just have to write your Python code in a `.py` file. Let's create a simple module named `math_operations` which contains some basic mathematical functions like addition, subtraction, etc.

Create a file named `math_operations.py` and put the following code in it:

```
# math_operations.py

def add(x, y):
    return x + y

def subtract(x, y):
    return x - y

def multiply(x, y):
    return x * y

def divide(x, y):
    if y != 0:
        return x / y
    else:
```

```
        return "Cannot divide by zero"
```

That's it! You've just created a Python module.

How to Use a Module

Using a module is just as easy as creating one. You just have to use the `import` statement. Open a new Python file and write:

```
import math_operations
result = math_operations.add(5, 3)
print(result)   # Output will be 8
```

Here, `math_operations` is the name of the module we want to import. Then, we can use its functions by referencing it as `math_operations.function_name`.

Importing Specific Functions

You can also import only specific functions from a module:

```
from math_operations import add, subtract

print(add(5, 3))   # Output will be 8
print(subtract(10, 3))   # Output will be 7
```

This way, you don't have to use the module name as a prefix when you call the function. But be cautious with this approach, especially when importing functions from different modules, as it can lead to function name clashes.

Alias in Modules

You can also use aliases to give a different name to the module or function when you import it.

```
import math_operations as mo
print(mo.add(5, 3))   # Output will be 8
```

Built-in Modules

Python comes with a bounty of built-in modules that offer functionalities for a range of different tasks. For instance, the os module provides a way of using operating system-dependent functionality like reading or writing to the file system. The math module offers mathematical operations and constants.

```
import os
import math

print(math.sqrt(16))   # Output will be 4.0
print(os.getcwd())   # Output will be the current working directory
```

Exercises

1. Create a module called string_operations that contains a function to reverse a string and another function to capitalize the first letter of each word in a string.

2. Import your string_operations module in another Python script and test the functions.

3. Create a module named file_operations. Include functions to read and write to a text file. Test these functions by reading and writing a sample text.

Let's get to work on these exercises, and I'll see you on the other side with solutions!

Solutions to the Exercises

Absolutely, let's break down the solutions for each exercise:

Solution for Exercise 1

You were asked to create a module named string_operations that has two functions: one to reverse a string and another to capitalize the first letter of each word in a string.

Here's how you can write the code in string_operations.py:

```python
# string_operations.py

def reverse_string(s):
    return s[::-1]

def capitalize_words(s):
    return ' '.join(word.capitalize() for word in s.split())
```

Solution for Exercise 2

Once your string_operations module is ready, you can import it into another Python script like this:

```python
import string_operations

# Test reverse_string function
result = string_operations.reverse_string('hello')
print(result)   # Output will be 'olleh'

# Test capitalize_words function
result = string_operations.capitalize_words('hello world')
print(result)   # Output will be 'Hello World'
```

Solution for Exercise 3

Create a module named file_operations and include functions to read and write text to a file. Here's your file_operations.py:

```python
# file_operations.py
```

```python
def write_to_file(filename, content):
    with open(filename, 'w') as f:
        f.write(content)


def read_from_file(filename):
    with open(filename, 'r') as f:
        return f.read()
```

To test the `file_operations` module, you can write the following in a new Python script:

```python
import file_operations

# Write content to a file
file_operations.write_to_file('sample.txt', 'Hello, world!')

# Read content from the file
print(file_operations.read_from_file('sample.txt'))
# Output will be 'Hello, world!'
```

And there you have it, solutions to all three exercises! You've successfully created and utilized modules in Python, and hopefully, you've got a solid understanding of the importance and usefulness of modules.

Chapter 9: Exception Handling

Intro to Exception Handling

This chapter is like your bulletproof vest when you're navigating the unpredictable world of programming. I mean, let's be real, errors are the unwanted guests at our programming party, right? They just show up, usually uninvited. But worry not! Python's exception handling mechanisms are here to save the day.

Why Even Handle Exceptions?

The first question that might pop up in your head is, why should we even bother? Well, unhandled errors are not just ugly; they can crash your program and result in an awful user experience. Handling errors gracefully ensures that your application can keep running, even when something unexpected happens. And believe me, unexpected things will happen.

The Basic Terminology

Before we go any further, let's get the jargon out of the way:

1. Exception: A disruptive event that occurs during the execution of a program, triggering a change in the normal flow of the program's instructions.

2.Throw/Raise: The act of creating an exception. Python does this for you when something goes awry.

3. Catch/Handle: Dealing with an exception that has been thrown.

4. Finally: A block of code that will execute no matter what, usually to clean up resources.

Got it? Good! Now let's move on.

Your First Exception

Okay, let's start with an example. Imagine you are trying to divide two numbers, and the user has input 0 as the divisor. An attempt to run this operation will result in a ZeroDivisionError. Here's a simplified code snippet:

```
# This will result in a ZeroDivisionError
result = 10 / 0
```

If you run this code, your program will crash and spit out an ugly traceback, leaving your user utterly confused. Not ideal, huh?

Try and Except

Enter Python's `try` and `except` blocks. These are the bread and butter of Python exception handling. Let's modify the code snippet:

```
try:
    result = 10 / 0
except ZeroDivisionError:
    print("Whoops! You can't divide by zero.")
```

See what happened? The `try` block "tries" to execute the code. If an exception occurs, the `except` block catches it and executes its code, instead of halting the program entirely.

Multiple Exceptions

Python lets you handle multiple exceptions differently. You can specify multiple `except` blocks to catch and handle each type of exception separately.

```python
try:
    # some code that can throw multiple exceptions
except ZeroDivisionError:
    print("Can't divide by zero")
except ValueError:
    print("Invalid input")
```

The Finally Block

The `finally` block is where you put any code that must execute, whether an exception was raised or not. This is a great place to close files, release resources, or do any other type of cleanup.

```python
try:
    # some code
except SomeException:
    # handle exception
finally:
    print("This will always run.")
```

Raise Your Own Exceptions

Not to be left behind, Python also allows you to raise your own exceptions using the `raise` keyword. For instance, if you're writing a function and you want to enforce some pre-conditions, you can throw a custom exception.

```python
def some_function(value):
    if value < 0:
        raise ValueError("Negative value detected!")
```

In this chapter, we'll go deeper into these mechanisms, explore different kinds of errors you might encounter, and learn advanced techniques to manage exceptions gracefully.

Exercise: Your First Exception Handler

1. Write a Python program that asks the user for two numbers and divides them. Use exception handling to catch a `ZeroDivisionError` and a `ValueError` (for non-numeric input).

75

2. Write a function that takes a filename as an argument and reads the content of the file. Use a `finally` block to ensure that the file is closed, whether an exception occurred or not.

Remember, the only predictable thing about software is its unpredictability. So, get ready to manage the unexpected effectively. Happy coding! ↻

Solutions to the Exercises

Exercise 1: Division with Exception Handling

Here, we'll write a Python program that asks the user for two numbers and then divides them. We will catch any `ZeroDivisionError` and `ValueError`.

```python
def divide_numbers():
    try:
        num1 = float(input("Enter the first number: "))
        num2 = float(input("Enter the second number: "))
        result = num1 / num2
        print(f"The result is {result}")
    except ZeroDivisionError:
        print("Whoops! You can't divide by zero.")
    except ValueError:
        print("Invalid input. Please enter a number.")


# Run the function to test it
divide_numbers()
```

Run the `divide_numbers` function, and it should handle both zero division and invalid inputs gracefully.

Exercise 2: File Reading with Finally Block

In this exercise, we will write a function that takes a filename as an argument and reads the content of the file. We'll use a `finally` block to make sure that the file gets closed, whether an exception occurred or not.

```python
def read_file(filename):
    try:
        file = open(filename, 'r')
        content = file.read()
        print(content)
    except FileNotFoundError:
        print(f"The file {filename} was not found.")
    finally:
```

```
        if 'file' in locals():
            file.close()
            print("The file has been closed.")

# Test the function
read_file("some_file.txt")
```

Make sure to create a file named "some_file.txt" with some text in it to test this function properly. If the file doesn't exist, the program will tell you so but still close any opened files.

Feel free to experiment more to get a stronger grip on exception handling in Python. Happy coding!

Absolutely, let's delve into the fascinating world of errors in Python.

_ *Understanding Errors*

What are Errors?

Let's get one thing straight: errors are not inherently bad. In fact, they serve as valuable checkpoints that tell you something's amiss in your code, acting almost like a built-in debugging assistant. Errors in Python can be broadly classified into two categories: Syntax Errors and Exceptions.

Syntax Errors

These are the first type of errors you'll likely encounter as a Python newbie. Syntax errors, often termed "parsing errors," occur when the Python interpreter can't understand your code. It's like the grammatical mistakes in a spoken language. Python will spit out an error message and highlight the part of the code that seems to be the issue.

Example:

```
# Missing closing parenthesis
print("Hello, world"
Running this would yield:
javascriptCopy code
SyntaxError: unexpected EOF while parsing
```

Exceptions

Even if your code is syntactically correct, it may still raise an error during execution, known as an Exception. Exceptions are more sneaky than Syntax Errors. They'll let you compile your program, only to disrupt it at runtime. Some common exceptions include `TypeError`, `ValueError`, `IndexError`, etc.

Example:

```
# Dividing by zero
result = 10 / 0
```

Running this code will produce:

```
vbnetCopy code
ZeroDivisionError: division by zero
```

Common Python Exceptions
- `ValueError`: Raised when a function receives an argument of the correct type but an inappropriate value.
- `TypeError`: Occurs when an operation or function is applied to an object of an inappropriate type.
- `IndexError`: Raised when you try to access an index that doesn't exist in a list.
- `KeyError`: Occurs when you try to access a dictionary key that doesn't exist.
- `FileNotFoundError`: Speaks for itself—happens when trying to open a file that doesn't exist.

Why Understanding Errors is Crucial
1. Faster Debugging: Knowing the type of error can drastically reduce debugging time.

2. Data Integrity: Unhandled errors can lead to inconsistent data states, which can be disastrous if you're working on something critical.

3. Improved User Experience: Handling errors gracefully allows you to provide more informative error messages to the end-users, making your application more robust and user-friendly.

Error Messages: Your Friend, Not Foe
Python error messages are quite descriptive, providing information about the type of error, where it occurred, and sometimes even what you can do to fix it. Always read them carefully; they are your first clue in the debugging process.

Format of a typical Python error message:
```
phpCopy code
Traceback (most recent call last):
  File "<filename>", line XX, in <module>
    <offending code>
<Error Type>: <Error Description>
```

Exercises
1. **Syntax Error Hunt**: Write a piece of code that deliberately contains a syntax error. Run the code and read the error message. Can you fix it?
2. **Exception Encounter**: Try dividing a number by zero and catch that specific exception to print a user-friendly error message.
3. **TypeError Test**: Create a function that adds two numbers, but pass one number and one string as parameters. Catch the `TypeError` and print a custom error message.

Solutions to the Exercises

Syntax Error Hunt

```
print("Hello, World!"
```

Fixed Code

78

```
print("Hello, World!")
```

Exception Encounter

```
try:
    result = 10 / 0
except ZeroDivisionError:
    print("You can't divide by zero!")
```

Output

```
rustCopy code
You can't divide by zero!
```

TypeError Test

```
def add_numbers(a, b):
    try:
        return a + b
    except TypeError:
        print("Oops! Both parameters should be numbers.")

add_numbers(5, "10")
```

Output

```
scssCopy code
Oops! Both parameters should be numbers.
```

Keep practicing these examples, and feel free to create your own. The more errors you encounter, the better you'll get at solving them!

Absolutely! Let's dive into the riveting world of "Try, Except, Finally: Managing Exceptions Gracefully." This sub-chapter promises to be an eye-opener for handling errors elegantly in Python. Errors are not necessarily a bad thing; they're just feedback mechanisms that help us make our code more resilient. So let's roll up our sleeves and get down to business!

Try, Except, Finally: A Closer Look

When things are sailing smoothly in your Python program, life is good. But what happens when things go south? What if your code encounters an error it didn't anticipate? Should the whole program crash and burn? Absolutely not! This is where the Try-Except-Finally block shines.

What is a Try-Except-Finally Block?

A Try-Except-Finally block is Python's built-in mechanism for exception handling. This block allows your program to "try" to execute some code and provides a safety net in case something goes wrong.

Here's the basic syntax for a Try-Except-Finally block:

```
try:
    # The code you 'try' to execute goes here.
except SomeSpecificError:
    # What to do if a specific error occurs.
except AnotherSpecificError:
    # What to do if another specific error occurs.
finally:
    # This code will run regardless of whether an error occurred or not.
```

The 'Try' Block

The `try` block encases the code that could potentially raise an error. It's like saying, "Let's give this a go, but be prepared for anything."

```
try:
    result = 10 / 2
except ZeroDivisionError:
    result = "Cannot divide by zero"
```

The 'Except' Block

The `except` block kicks in when an error is encountered in the `try` block. You can even specify the type of error to catch, giving you laser-focused control over error handling. Here's an example that catches a `ValueError`:

```
try:
    user_input = int(input("Enter a number: "))
except ValueError:
    print("That's not a valid number!")
```

The 'Finally' Block

Think of the `finally` block as your program's cleanup crew. This block is executed no matter what—whether an error is raised or not. Here's a simple example:

```
try:
    print("Trying to read a file.")
    file = open('nonexistent_file.txt', 'r')
except FileNotFoundError:
    print("Oops, file not found.")
```

```
finally:
    print("This will execute no matter what.")
```

Nesting Try-Except Blocks
You can also nest Try-Except blocks for more granular control. This is particularly useful when dealing with loops or conditional statements.

```
try:
    for i in [2, 1.5, 0, 3]:
        try:
            print(10 / i)
        except ZeroDivisionError:
            print("Can't divide by zero!")
finally:
    print("Loop completed.")
```

Best Practices
1. Be Specific with Exceptions: Always specify the exception type rather than using a generic `except` block. This makes your code more readable and easier to debug.

2. Don't Swallow Exceptions: Never leave the `except` block empty. Always either handle the exception or log it for debugging later.

3. Resource Cleanup: Use the `finally` block for any cleanup activity, like closing files or releasing resources.

Practical Exercises
1. Create a program that asks the user for two numbers and divides them. Handle any division errors gracefully.

2. Read a file that doesn't exist and print a friendly error message.

3. Use nested Try-Except blocks in a for-loop that iterates through a list of numbers and string, trying to cast each as an integer.

The best code is not the code that never fails; it's the code that knows how to fail gracefully.

Absolutely! Let's dive into the solutions for those exercises so you can get hands-on experience with Python's exception-handling mechanisms.

Solution to the Exercises

Solution to Exercise 1
Objective: Create a program that asks the user for two numbers and divides them. Handle any division errors gracefully.

```
try:
```

```
    num1 = float(input("Enter the first number: "))
    num2 = float(input("Enter the second number: "))
    result = num1 / num2
    print(f"The result of {num1} divided by {num2} is {result}.")
except ZeroDivisionError:
    print("Sorry, you can't divide by zero!")
except ValueError:
    print("Oops! That's not a valid number.")
```

In this exercise, we have two `except` blocks. The first one catches a `ZeroDivisionError`, and the second one catches a `ValueError` for invalid input.

Solution to Exercise 2

Objective: Read a file that doesn't exist and print a friendly error message.

```
try:
    with open('nonexistent_file.txt', 'r') as file:
        print(file.read())
except FileNotFoundError:
    print("Oops, file not found.")
```

Here, the `FileNotFoundError` is caught, and a friendly message is displayed to the user.

Solution to Exercise 3

Objective: Use nested Try-Except blocks in a for-loop that iterates through a list of numbers and strings, trying to cast each as an integer.

```
my_list = [2, "3", 0, "apple", 4]

try:
    for item in my_list:
        try:
            print(int(item))
        except ValueError:
            print(f"Can't convert {item} to an integer.")
except Exception as e:
    print(f"An unexpected error occurred: {e}")
finally:
    print("Loop completed.")
```

In this nested Try-Except block, we first try to iterate through the list `my_list`. Inside the for-loop, we have another Try-Except block that tries to convert each item to an integer.

Remember, it's not just about writing code that works; it's about writing code that works well, even when things go wrong.

Chapter 10: File Handling in Python: The ABCs of Reading, Writing, and Managing Files

You've dabbled with variables, looped through lists, and crafted some classy classes. Now, it's time to bring your Python programs into the real world. How, you ask? By mastering file handling!

File handling in Python allows your programs to connect with external files, which can be text files, databases, spreadsheets, or even web data. This chapter will guide you through the ins and outs of file handling, transforming you into a Pythonic file whisperer. You'll learn not just how to read and write files, but also how to manage them effectively.

Learning Objectives

- Understand what file handling is and why it's crucial.
- Become familiar with various file types and how to handle them.
- Learn how to read from and write to files.
- Grasp how to manage large files without overwhelming your system.

So, let's get cracking! Reading and writing files is a core skill for any programmer, and in Python, it's a piece of cake—or should we say, a slice of Pi!

Questions

- What are the three primary uses of file handling in programming?
- Can you list three file formats that Python can interact with?

Ready to dive deeper? In the next section, we'll discuss various file types you'll encounter while programming in Python.

Types of File

Alright, let's get to know the various types of files we can tango with in Python. Generally speaking, files fall into two broad categories:

1. Text Files: These are human-readable files containing text and follow a specific encoding like ASCII or UTF-8. Think `.txt`, `.csv`, `.html`, or even `.py` files. Yes, Python source code files are also text files!

2. Binary Files: Not human-readable, these files contain a sequence of bytes. Image files like `.jpg`, `.png`, and executable `.exe`, or even database `.db` files fall under this category.

Why the Distinction Matters

You might be thinking, "So what? A file is a file, right?" Ah, but the way you handle these two types is different. For example, while reading a text file, you usually read it line by line or character by character. Binary files, on the other hand, require you to read them byte by byte.

Common File Extensions

- **Text Files**: `.txt`, `.csv`, `.json`, `.xml`, `.html`, `.md`
- **Binary Files**: `.jpg`, `.png`, `.gif`, `.pdf`, `.db`, `.mp3`, `.mp4`

What About Mixed Files?

Good question! Some file formats, like `.pdf`, can actually contain both text and binary data. However, Python libraries that handle such files usually abstract away the complexity, so you won't have to worry much about it.

Exercises

1. List down three text file formats and two binary file formats.
2. What is the primary difference between text and binary files in terms of how they are read?

Opening a File: The First Step in the File-Handling Dance

The Basics of `open()`

Alright, so you've got a file and you're ready to do some work with it. The first step? Opening that baby up. In Python, the `open()` function is your go-to for this operation. It's like the key to your file's front door. The syntax is simple:

```
file_object = open('filename', 'mode')
```

- `filename`: The name of the file you want to open. Don't forget to include the file extension like `.txt` or `.csv`.
- `mode`: This tells Python what you plan to do with the file. Are you reading it (`'r'`), writing to it (`'w'`), or doing something else?

Common Modes

1. `'r'`: Read mode. Opens the file for reading.
2. `'w'`: Write mode. Opens the file for writing (and creates it if it doesn't exist).
3. `'a'`: Append mode. Opens the file for writing but keeps the existing data and adds new data to the end.
4. `'b'`: Binary mode. Used with other modes like `'rb'` or `'wb'` to read or write binary files.
   You can combine modes, too. For example, `'r+'` allows you to both read and write.

Examples

```
# Opening a text file for reading
file_read = open('example.txt', 'r')


# Opening a text file for writing
file_write = open('example_write.txt', 'w')


# Opening a binary file for reading
file_bin_read = open('example.jpg', 'rb')
```

A Word of Caution:

Be careful when using `'w'` mode. If the file already exists, it will overwrite it. Ouch!

The Big Responsibility

Remember, once you open a file, you need to close it later, or else it's like leaving your front door wide open. We'll discuss closing files in a later section, but it's crucial enough to warrant an early mention.

Exercises

1. Write a Python script to open a file named `my_text.txt` in read mode.
2. Write a Python script to open a binary file named `my_image.jpg` in read mode.
3. What mode would you use to open a file if you wanted to both read and write to it?

Solutions to the Exercises

Exercise 1: Write a Python script to open a file named `my_text.txt` in read mode.

Here's how you can do it:

```python
# Solution to Exercise 1
try:
    file = open('my_text.txt', 'r')
    print("File opened successfully!")
    # Remember to close the file
    file.close()
except FileNotFoundError:
    print("File not found.")
```

By using `try` and `except`, you're taking into account the possibility that the file might not exist. This is good practice for error handling.

Exercise 2: Write a Python script to open a binary file named `my_image.jpg` in read mode.

Here it is:

```python
# Solution to Exercise 2
try:
    file = open('my_image.jpg', 'rb')
    print("Binary file opened successfully!")
    # Remember to close the file
    file.close()
except FileNotFoundError:
    print("File not found.")
```

Again, we use `try` and `except` for robust error handling.

Exercise 3: What mode would you use to open a file if you wanted to both read and write to it?

The answer is `'r+'`. This mode allows you to both read and write to the file.

And there you have it—solutions to all the exercises. By now, you should be comfortable with opening different types of files in Python. Next up, we'll learn how to properly close these files. Stay tuned!

Closing a File

Just like you wouldn't leave your front door wide open when you go out, you shouldn't leave a file open in your program. Closing a file frees up the resources tied to that file and ensures that all the data is written to the disk. Let's dive into why it's so crucial and how to do it.

The `close()` Method

Python makes it quite easy to close a file. All you have to do is invoke the `close()` method on the file object, like so:

```
# Open the file
file = open('my_text_file.txt', 'r')


# Do operations...


# Close the file
file.close()
```

Simple, isn't it? But do you wonder why this matters? Let's see.

Why is Closing Files Important?

1. Resource Allocation: Every open file eats up system resources. If you have a large number of files open, or if a single file is large, you might run into resource limitations.

2. Data Loss: Sometimes, especially when writing data to a file, the data is buffered. This means it's temporarily stored in memory. Closing the file ensures that the data is flushed from the buffer to the actual file, preventing data loss.

3. File Corruption: Leaving files open increases the risk of them being corrupted, especially if you're writing to them.

4. Concurrency Issues: In a multi-user environment, not closing a file might result in inconsistencies as different users try to access it simultaneously.

When Does Python Close Files Automatically?

Python does try to close files automatically when the file object is garbage collected. But depending on your Python environment and how your code is structured, you can't be 100% sure when that will happen. So it's always best to close files explicitly.

Exercises

1. Open a file, write some text into it, and then close it. Check the file to see if the text is saved.

2. Open a file, read its content, and close it. Try reading from the file again after you've closed it and see what happens.

Solutions to the Exercises

Exercise 1: Writing and Closing

In this exercise, you were asked to open a file, write some text into it, and then close it. The objective was to verify if the text is saved in the file.

```python
# Solution to Exercise 1
# Open the file in write mode
with open('exercise1.txt', 'w') as file:
    file.write("Hello, this is Exercise 1.")
```

Once you run this code, check the directory where your Python file is saved. You'll find a new text file named exercise1.txt, and it will contain the text "Hello, this is Exercise 1."

Exercise 2: Reading and Closing

In this exercise, you had to open a file, read its content, and then close it. Then, try reading from the file again after you've closed it to see what happens.

```python
# Solution to Exercise 2
# Open the file in read mode
with open('exercise1.txt', 'r') as file:
    content = file.read()
    print("Content before closing: ", content)

# Try to read the file after closing it
try:
    print("Trying to read after closing: ", file.read())
except ValueError as e:
    print(f"An error occurred: {e}")
```

In this example, I used the with statement to open the file, which automatically closes it after the nested block of code. After the with block, trying to read the file again raises a ValueError, indicating that the file is closed and can't be read from anymore.

TextIOWrapper Class: Your Guide to Stream Operations

When you're working with files in Python, you're likely to encounter a TextIOWrapper object. Now, what the heck is that? Don't worry! By the end of this section, you'll be quite familiar with this tongue-twister of a term.

What is TextIOWrapper?

In simple words, `TextIOWrapper` is a class that provides methods to read and write text-based files—like your `.txt` or `.csv` files. Whenever you open a text file using Python's built-in `open()` function, you're actually creating a `TextIOWrapper` object.

How Does It Work?

Let's break it down with some basic code.

```python
# Opening a text file
file = open('my_text_file.txt', 'r')
print(type(file))
```

Run this code, and you'll see:

```
<class '_io.TextIOWrapper'>
```

That's right! The `file` variable is an instance of the `TextIOWrapper` class. But what can you do with it?

Methods and Attributes

The `TextIOWrapper` class has some super handy methods and attributes. Let's delve into a few:

- `read()`: Reads and returns the content of the file as a string.
- `readline()`: Reads a single line from the file.
- `writelines(lines)`: Writes a list of lines to the file.
- `name`: Gets the name of the file you're working with.

Here's a mini-demo:

```python
# Mini-demo
file = open('my_text_file.txt', 'r')

# Reading the whole file
print(file.read())

# Finding out the file name
print(file.name)

# Don't forget to close the file
file.close()
```

Safety First!

As much as we're excited about reading and writing files, we should also be cautious.
1. Always close the file: After you're done with your file operations, close the file using file.close() to free up resources.
2. Error Handling: Use try, except, and finally to handle file errors gracefully.

Here's how you can do it:

```
# Error Handling with TextIOWrapper
try:
    file = open('my_nonexistent_file.txt', 'r')
except FileNotFoundError:
    print("File not found!")
finally:
    file.close()
```

Exercises

Exercise 1: Open a text file and read the first line. Print the type of the object returned.

Exercise 2: Use `writelines()` to write multiple lines to a text file. What type of argument does `writelines()` accept?

Exercise 3: How would you handle a situation where the file you're trying to open doesn't exist? Show this with code.

Solutions to the Exercises

Solution to Exercise 1

The aim is to open a text file and read the first line. Then print the type of the object returned.

```
# Open the text file
file = open('my_text_file.txt', 'r')

# Read the first line
first_line = file.readline()

# Print the type of the object returned
print(type(first_line))

# Close the file
file.close()
```

When you run this code, you'll see:

```
<class 'str'>
```

The `readline()` method returns a string.

Solution to Exercise 2:

The goal is to use `writelines()` to write multiple lines to a text file. The function accepts an iterable, like a list of strings.

90

```
# Open the text file in write mode
file = open('my_text_file.txt', 'w')

# List of lines to write
lines = ['Hello, world!', 'How are you?']

# Add newline character to each line
lines = [line + '\n' for line in lines]

# Use writelines() to write the lines
file.writelines(lines)

# Close the file
file.close()
```

This will write the list of lines to your text file.

Solution to Exercise 3

The objective is to handle a situation where the file you're trying to open doesn't exist.

```
# Attempt to open a non-existent file
try:
    file = open('my_nonexistent_file.txt', 'r')
except FileNotFoundError:
    print('File not found!')
finally:
    try:
        file.close()
    except NameError:
        print('File was never opened.')
```

This code will catch the `FileNotFoundError` and inform you that the file was not found.

_ *Other File Operations*

Writing Data to the Text File

Let's dive right in by learning how to write data into a text file. This is a key aspect of file handling in Python. You can use the `write()` method to write strings directly into a file.

Example

```
# Open the file in write mode
with open("my_file.txt", "w") as file:
    file.write("Hello, world!")
```

In this example, the `with` statement automatically closes the file for us after writing to it.

Exercise

Create a text file and write "Hello, Python learners!" into it. Then open it to check if the text was saved correctly.

Reading Data from a Text File

Reading data is equally straightforward. You use the `read()` method for this.

Example

```
# Open the file in read mode
with open("my_file.txt", "r") as file:
    content = file.read()
    print(content)
```

Exercise

Create a text file, write some data to it, and then read it back into your Python program.

Reading Large Files

For large files, reading the entire file at once can be memory-inefficient. You can read the file line-by-line using a for-loop to save memory.

Example

```
# Reading large files line-by-line
with open("large_file.txt", "r") as file:
    for line in file:
        print(line.strip())
```

Exercise:

Create a large text file (around 100 lines) and read it line-by-line using a Python program.

Appending Data to the Text File

Sometimes, you need to add data to an existing file without overwriting the previous data. This is where the append (`a`) mode comes in.

Example

```
# Open the file in append mode
with open("my_file.txt", "a") as file:
    file.write("\nThis is an appended line.")
```

Exercise

Write a Python program to append "Happy Learning!" to a pre-existing text file.

Working with Files Using the `with` Statement

The `with` statement is a context manager that simplifies the process of opening and closing files. Always prefer using `with` for more reliable and clean code.

Example

```
with open("my_file.txt", "r") as file:
```

```
    print(file.read())
```

Exercise
Open a text file using the `with` statement, write something into it, and then read it back.

Reading and Writing Binary Data
Sometimes, you might have to work with binary files, such as images or audio files. You can use the `rb` and `wb` modes for reading and writing binary data, respectively.

Example

```
# Copying an image file
with open("source.jpg", "rb") as src_file:
    data = src_file.read()


with open("destination.jpg", "wb") as dest_file:
    dest_file.write(data)
```

Exercise
Try reading and writing a binary file (like an image) using a Python program.

Solutions to the Exercises

Exercise for Writing Data to the Text File

```
with open("exercise_file.txt", "w") as file:
    file.write("Hello, Python learners!")
```

After running this code, you can manually open `exercise_file.txt` to ensure that the text "Hello, Python learners!" has been written correctly.

Exercise for Reading Data from a Text File
Firstly, you can use the previous exercise code to write some data to the file. Then, you can read it back like so:

```
with open("exercise_file.txt", "r") as file:
    content = file.read()
    print(content)
```

This should print "Hello, Python learners!" to the console.

Exercise for Reading Large Files
For this exercise, you can manually create a large text file or use Python to generate one. To read it line-by-line, you can use:

```
with open("large_file.txt", "r") as file:
```

```
    for line in file:
        print(line.strip())
```

Exercise for Appending Data to the Text File:

```
with open("exercise_file.txt", "a") as file:
    file.write("\nHappy Learning!")
```

After executing this code, the file exercise_file.txt should contain the original text plus the newly appended "Happy Learning!".

Exercise for Working with Files Using the with Statement:

You can combine writing and reading within the same with statement as follows:

```
with open("exercise_with_file.txt", "w+") as file:
    file.write("This is a new line.")
    file.seek(0)
    print(file.read())
```

This code writes "This is a new line." to the file and then reads it back, printing it to the console.

Exercise for Reading and Writing Binary Data

To copy an image, you can use:

```
with open("source.jpg", "rb") as src_file:
    data = src_file.read()

with open("destination.jpg", "wb") as dest_file:
    dest_file.write(data)
```

This reads an image source.jpg and creates a new copy named destination.jpg.

Feel free to run these solutions to see how they work and compare them with your own solutions.

Chapter 11: Object Oriented Programming (OOP) in Python

Procedural Programming in Python

Before we delve into the realm of Object-Oriented Programming (OOP), let's first get a strong grip on Procedural Programming, which is the fundamental building block of Python and many other languages. You've probably already been doing Procedural Programming without realizing it, so let's break it down and understand what it's all about.

What is Procedural Programming?

Procedural Programming is a paradigm or a pattern in which programming tasks are broken down into procedures, also known as functions or routines. Essentially, it's all about writing a list of instructions for the computer to perform. Each procedure performs a specific task and is often reusable, making your code more efficient and less repetitive.

Structure of Procedural Programs

In a Procedural Program, the flow of execution is usually top-to-bottom, starting from the initial function call, such as `main()` in some languages, and proceeding through various function calls. The program's state is maintained through variables, which can be global or local in scope.

```python
# A simple procedural program to calculate the area of a circle
import math

def calculate_area(radius):
    area = math.pi * (radius ** 2)
    return area

def main():
    r = 5  # radius of the circle
    area_of_circle = calculate_area(r)
    print(f"The area of the circle with radius {r} is {area_of_circle}")

if __name__ == "__main__":
    main()
```

Functions, The Core of Procedural Programming

The function is the most crucial element in Procedural Programming. Functions package your code into reusable blocks, making it modular and easier to maintain. Python has both built-in functions like `print()`, `len()`, and the capability for you to define your functions.

95

Variable Scope and Lifetime

Understanding variable scope and lifetime is key in Procedural Programming. Local variables exist only within the function where they are declared, while global variables can be accessed throughout the entire program. However, be cautious when using global variables, as they can make the program harder to debug.

```python
x = 10   # global variable

def show():
    y = 5   # local variable
    print(x, y)

show()
```

Loops and Conditional Statements

The usage of loops (`for`, `while`) and conditional statements (`if`, `elif`, `else`) plays a vital role in controlling the flow of the program. These are used to execute different sets of instructions based on conditions or repeatedly as long as a condition is met.

Error Handling

A Procedural Program should also handle errors gracefully, usually through `try`, `except` blocks, to continue the program execution or terminate it in a controlled way.

```python
try:
    # some code
except SomeError:
    # error handling code
```

Advantages of Procedural Programming

1. **Simplicity:** Since the program is a series of functions with clear inputs and outputs, it's often easier to understand.
2. **Reusability:** Functions can be reused across different parts of the program or even in other programs.
3. **Efficiency:** Given the modular approach, it's generally easier to optimize specific parts of a Procedural Program.

Limitations

1. **Scalability:** For large and complex programs, managing a Procedural Program can become challenging.
2. **Global Data:** The use of global variables makes it susceptible to bugs and issues related to data integrity.

3. **Lack of Real-world Modeling:** Real-world problems are often not procedural but rather a collection of entities that interact with each other, which is better modeled by Object-Oriented Programming.

Exercises

1. Write a function to calculate the factorial of a given number.
2. Create a function to sort an array of numbers in ascending order.
3. Develop a procedural program to read a text file and count the number of words in it.

Understanding Procedural Programming is like learning basic arithmetic before tackling algebra or calculus. Now that we've covered the basics, you're better equipped to dive into the more complex, yet more powerful, paradigm of Object-Oriented Programming (OOP) in the following sections.

Solutions to the Exercises

Exercise 1: Write a function to calculate the factorial of a given number.
Here's how you could do it using a loop:

```
def factorial(n):
    result = 1
    for i in range(1, n + 1):
        result *= i
    return result

print(factorial(5))   # Output should be 120
```

Or using recursion:

```
def factorial_recursive(n):
    if n == 1:
        return 1
    return n * factorial_recursive(n-1)

print(factorial_recursive(5))   # Output should be 120
```

Exercise 2: Create a function to sort an array of numbers in ascending order.
You could do it with a simple sorting algorithm like bubble sort:

```
def bubble_sort(arr):
    n = len(arr)
    for i in range(n):
```

```
        for j in range(0, n-i-1):
            if arr[j] > arr[j+1]:
                arr[j], arr[j+1] = arr[j+1], arr[j]
    return arr

print(bubble_sort([64, 25, 12, 22, 11]))   # Output should be [11, 12, 22, 25, 64]
```

Exercise 3: Develop a procedural program to read a text file and count the number of words in it.

Here's a simple way to do it:

```
def count_words(filename):
    try:
        with open(filename, 'r') as file:
            text = file.read()
            words = text.split()
            return len(words)
    except FileNotFoundError:
        return "File not found"

print(count_words("example.txt"))   # Replace "example.txt" with the path to your text
file
```

_Object-Oriented Programming (OOP)

Alright, we've spent some good time on procedural programming, and I hope you're feeling confident about it. Now, let's switch gears and dive into the much-anticipated Object-Oriented Programming, often abbreviated as OOP. This is another paradigm for organizing your code, and it comes with its own set of rules, concepts, and benefits.

The Philosophy of OOP

OOP is based on the idea that everything can be modeled as an object. Think of objects as the building blocks of applications. Just like in the real world, where objects like a pen, a cup, or a computer have attributes (color, size, shape) and behaviors (write, hold water, compute), objects in programming have attributes (data) and behaviors (methods).

Why Use OOP?

The primary advantage of OOP is that it encourages code reusability and makes the code more organized, easier to test, and maintain. It brings the concept of inheritance, encapsulation, and polymorphism into play. We'll touch on these juicy terms shortly.

Class: The Blueprint

In OOP, the term "class" refers to a blueprint for creating objects. A class defines what attributes an object should have and what actions it can perform. Once a class is defined, you can instantiate multiple objects from it, just like you can construct many houses from the same blueprint.

```python
class Dog:
    def __init__(self, name):
        self.name = name


    def bark(self):
        print("Woof, woof!")
```

Here, we've defined a simple `Dog` class. The `__init__` method is special; it's called a constructor and initializes the object when you create it. The `self` keyword represents the instance (object) itself.

Instantiating Objects

Once the class is defined, creating objects is straightforward:

```python
my_dog = Dog("Fido")
my_dog.bark()   # Output: Woof, woof!
```

Encapsulation: Data Hiding

In OOP, you can restrict direct access to attributes, a concept known as encapsulation. By doing so, you're hiding the internal state of the object and requiring all interaction to be performed through the object's methods.

```python
class BankAccount:
    def __init__(self, balance=0):
        self.__balance = balance


    def deposit(self, amount):
        self.__balance += amount


    def get_balance(self):
        return self.__balance
```

Notice the double underscores before the `balance` attribute. It makes the attribute private, meaning it can't be accessed directly from outside the class.

Inheritance: Code Reusability

One of the strongest points of OOP is the concept of inheritance, which allows you to create a new class based on an existing class. The new class inherits attributes and behaviors from the existing class.

```python
class Animal:
    def make_sound(self):
        print("Some generic sound")
```

```
class Dog(Animal):
    def make_sound(self):
        print("Woof, woof!")
```

Here, `Dog` is a subclass of `Animal` and overrides the `make_sound` method.

Polymorphism: One Interface, Multiple Behaviors

Polymorphism allows objects of different classes to be treated as objects of a common superclass. In simple terms, it enables one interface to be used for different data types.

```
def animal_sound(animal):
    animal.make_sound()

my_animal = Animal()
my_dog = Dog()

animal_sound(my_animal)   # Output: Some generic sound
animal_sound(my_dog)   # Output: Woof, woof!
```

Exercises

1. Create a class named `Car`. Add methods for `start`, `accelerate`, and `stop`.
2. Implement encapsulation in the `Car` class by making its attributes private.
3. Create a subclass of `Car` named `ElectricCar`. Override the `accelerate` method to display a message that it's accelerating silently.

These exercises will help solidify your understanding of Object-Oriented Programming. Happy coding!

Exercise Solutions

Let's jump right into the solutions for the exercises given in the Object-Oriented Programming sub-chapter.

Exercise 1: Creating the `Car` Class

You were asked to create a class named `Car` with methods for `start`, `accelerate`, and `stop`. Here's one way to implement it:

```
class Car:
    def start(self):
        print("Starting the car.")

    def accelerate(self):
```

```
        print("Accelerating the car.")

    def stop(self):
        print("Stopping the car.")
```

You can test this class as follows:

```
my_car = Car()
my_car.start()
my_car.accelerate()
my_car.stop()
```

Exercise 2: Implementing Encapsulation

In this exercise, you were supposed to implement encapsulation by making the attributes of the Car class private. We can use the double underscore prefix to make attributes private.

```
class Car:
    def __init__(self):
        self.__speed = 0

    def start(self):
        self.__speed = 20
        print(f"Starting the car. Speed is {self.__speed} mph.")

    def accelerate(self):
        self.__speed += 20
        print(f"Accelerating. Speed is now {self.__speed} mph.")

    def stop(self):
        self.__speed = 0
        print(f"Stopping the car. Speed is now {self.__speed} mph.")
```

Exercise 3: Create a Subclass ElectricCar

Finally, let's create a subclass of Car called ElectricCar and override the accelerate method.

```
class ElectricCar(Car):
    def accelerate(self):
        print("Accelerating silently.")
You can test this subclass as follows:

my_electric_car = ElectricCar()
my_electric_car.start()
my_electric_car.accelerate()
my_electric_car.stop()
```

Great job getting through these exercises! They should help you internalize the OOP concepts we've discussed. Stay tuned for more advanced topics and exercises in the coming subchapters!

Objects and Classes in Python

In the previous section, we scratched the surface of Object-Oriented Programming (OOP) in Python. We learned the essence of OOP and compared it to Procedural Programming. Now, it's time to delve deeper into the heart of OOP: **Objects and Classes**. This subchapter will elaborate on the foundation, unravel the terms in depth, and explain the core components that make OOP an effective programming paradigm.

What are Objects?

Think of an object as a mini-program or a unit of a program. Objects hold both data (attributes) and code (methods) that act on the data. They embody a higher level of abstraction, encapsulating properties and behaviors that belong together. When you create an object, you are essentially creating an instance of a class, which we'll get to in a moment.

In Python, everything is an object. Even primitive data types like integers and strings are objects. This means you can use methods with them.

```python
# Example with a string object
text = "hello"
print(text.upper())   # Outputs 'HELLO'
```

What are Classes?

Classes are the blueprints for creating objects. A single class can create multiple objects, just as a single blueprint can be used to construct multiple houses. Classes define what properties and methods its objects should have, but it doesn't hold any values for them.

```python
class Dog:
    def __init__(self, name, breed):
        self.name = name
        self.breed = breed

    def bark(self):
        print("Woof, woof!")
```

In the above example, Dog is a class. It has an __init__ method that initializes the object and a method called bark.

Creating Objects (Instantiation)

Creating an object from a class is known as "instantiation." Let's create an object of the Dog class.

```python
my_dog = Dog("Buddy", "Golden Retriever")
```

Here, `my_dog` is an object or instance of the `Dog` class. We passed the name "Buddy" and the breed "Golden Retriever" as arguments during the instantiation.

Accessing Attributes and Methods

After creating an object, you can access its attributes and methods using the dot notation.

```python
print(my_dog.name)   # Outputs 'Buddy'
print(my_dog.breed)  # Outputs 'Golden Retriever'
my_dog.bark()   # Outputs 'Woof, woof!'
```

Constructors and Destructors

The `__init__` method we've seen is a constructor method. It gets called when you create a new object. Python also has a destructor method named `__del__`, which gets executed when an object is destroyed.

```python
class Dog:
    def __init__(self, name):
        print(f"{name} is born.")

    def __del__(self):
        print(f"{self.name} is destroyed.")
```

The `self` Parameter

You might have noticed the `self` parameter in all the class methods. It refers to the instance of the class and gets passed implicitly when you call a method on an object. It's not a keyword; you could technically name it anything, but it's best practice to stick to `self`.

Exercises:

1. Create a class `Person` with attributes `name` and `age`. Add a method that prints "Hello, my name is [name], and I am [age] years old."

2. Create a class `Rectangle` with attributes `length` and `width`. Add methods to calculate the area and perimeter of the rectangle.

3. Create a class `BankAccount` with attributes `account_number` and `balance`. Add methods for depositing, withdrawing, and checking the balance.

Remember, understanding Objects and Classes is like learning the alphabet before writing essays. Master these fundamentals, and you'll find the more advanced OOP concepts easier to grasp. In the next sections, we will continue to build upon this foundational knowledge, exploring more advanced features of Python's OOP capabilities.

Solutions to the Execises

Exercise 1: Person Class

```python
class Person:
    def __init__(self, name, age):
```

```
            self.name = name
            self.age = age


    def introduce(self):
        print(f"Hello, my name is {self.name}, and I am {self.age} years old.")


# Test the class
john = Person("John", 25)
john.introduce()
```

Exercise 2: Rectangle Class

```
class Rectangle:
    def __init__(self, length, width):
        self.length = length
        self.width = width


    def area(self):
        return self.length * self.width


    def perimeter(self):
        return 2 * (self.length + self.width)


# Test the class
rect1 = Rectangle(5, 4)
print(f"The area of the rectangle is {rect1.area()}.")
print(f"The perimeter of the rectangle is {rect1.perimeter()}.")
```

Exercise 3: BankAccount Class

```
class BankAccount:
    def __init__(self, account_number, balance=0):
        self.account_number = account_number
        self.balance = balance


    def deposit(self, amount):
        self.balance += amount
        print(f"Deposited ${amount}. Current balance: ${self.balance}.")


    def withdraw(self, amount):
        if amount > self.balance:
            print("Insufficient funds.")
            return
```

```
        self.balance -= amount
        print(f"Withdrew ${amount}. Current balance: ${self.balance}.")


    def check_balance(self):
        print(f"Current balance: ${self.balance}.")

# Test the class
account1 = BankAccount(12345, 100)
account1.deposit(50)
account1.withdraw(30)
account1.check_balance()
```

These solutions illustrate how to define and manipulate classes and their objects in Python. Each class is designed to encapsulate specific attributes and methods related to the entity it represents. Feel free to run the code snippets to see how each class works in practice.

Passing Objects as Arguments to Functions

Here, we're going to dive into the concept of passing objects as arguments to functions. You've learned about variables, data types, and functions. But what happens when you combine these? Well, you get a technique that brings immense flexibility to your coding. So, sit tight and get ready for an interesting journey.

Learning Objectives

- Understanding the difference between passing by reference and by value.
- How to pass different types of objects to functions.
- Learn best practices for modifying objects within functions.

Passing by Reference vs. Passing by Value

First off, it's crucial to understand that in Python, all arguments are passed by object reference. This is different from languages like C++, where you can also pass by value. What does this mean? It means that if you modify the object you pass into a function, the changes persist even after the function execution is completed.

```
# Example: Passing by Reference
def modify_list(lst):
    lst.append(10)


my_list = [1, 2, 3]
modify_list(my_list)
print(my_list)  # Output: [1, 2, 3, 10]
```

In the above example, the list `my_list` gets modified inside the function `modify_list`. This modification persists, as demonstrated by the print statement.

Passing Immutable and Mutable Objects

Mutable objects like lists, dictionaries, and sets can be altered within functions. Immutable objects like strings, tuples, and numbers can't be changed.

```python
# Example: Passing Immutable Object
def modify_string(strng):
    strng += " World!"

my_str = "Hello"
modify_string(my_str)
print(my_str)    # Output: Hello
```

Even though we tried to modify `my_str` in the function `modify_string`, it remained the same. This is because strings in Python are immutable.

Exercises

1. Create a function that takes a list and doubles each of its elements. Test it with a list of numbers.
2. Create a function that takes a dictionary and doubles the values associated with each key.

Best Practices

- Be cautious when modifying mutable objects in functions.
- Clearly document any side-effects a function might have on the objects passed into it.
- Use return values when the intention is to create a modified copy of the data, rather than altering the original object.

Solutions to the Exercises

1. Doubling list elements:

```python
def double_elements(lst):
    for i in range(len(lst)):
        lst[i] *= 2

my_list = [1, 2, 3]
double_elements(my_list)
print(my_list)    # Output: [2, 4, 6]
```

2. Doubling dictionary values:

```
def double_values(dct):
    for key in dct:
        dct[key] *= 2

my_dict = {'a': 1, 'b': 2}
double_values(my_dict)
print(my_dict)   # Output: {'a': 2, 'b': 4}
```

_Deep Dive on Inheritance

If you've ever wondered how to create a new class that's based on an existing class but with some extras or modifications, then this section is for you.

Learning Objectives
- Understand the concept of inheritance in OOP.
- Learn how to create a subclass and override methods.
- Master the use of super() to extend functionality.

The Basics of Inheritance

Inheritance enables a new class, called a subclass, to inherit attributes and behavior (methods) from an existing class, known as the superclass. It's a way to promote code reusability and establish relationships between classes.

```
# Example: Simple Inheritance
class Animal:
    def make_sound(self):
        print("Some generic animal sound")

class Dog(Animal):
    pass

dog = Dog()
dog.make_sound()   # Output: Some generic animal sound
```

In this example, the Dog class inherits the make_sound method from the Animal class. Simple, isn't it?

Overriding Methods

One of the key features of inheritance is that the subclass can provide its own version of a method that's already defined in its superclass. This is known as overriding.

```
# Example: Method Overriding
class Cat(Animal):
    def make_sound(self):
        print("Meow")
```

```
cat = Cat()
cat.make_sound()   # Output: Meow
```

In this example, the `Cat` class overrides the `make_sound` method from its superclass `Animal`.

Using `super()` to Extend Functionality

Sometimes, you want to add some functionality to an existing method from the superclass. That's when `super()` comes to your rescue.

```
# Example: Using super()
class Bird(Animal):
    def make_sound(self):
        super().make_sound()
        print("And also, tweet tweet")

bird = Bird()
bird.make_sound()
# Output:
# Some generic animal sound
# And also, tweet tweet
```

Exercises

1. Create a `Vehicle` class with methods for starting and stopping. Create a `Car` subclass that overrides these methods and adds a `play_radio` method.
2. Create a `Shape` class with a method to calculate the area. Create `Square` and `Circle` subclasses with their own area calculation methods.

Best Practices

- Always use the `super()` function when you override methods and want to extend their functionality.
- Avoid overriding built-in Python methods unless you have a very good reason.
- Make sure to follow the Liskov Substitution Principle, which essentially states that objects of a superclass should be replaceable with objects of a subclass without affecting the correctness of the program.

Solutions to the Exercises

1. Vehicle and Car classes:

```
class Vehicle:
    def start(self):
        print("Starting vehicle")

    def stop(self):
        print("Stopping vehicle")
```

```python
class Car(Vehicle):
    def start(self):
        super().start()
        print("Starting car engine")

    def stop(self):
        super().stop()
        print("Stopping car engine")

    def play_radio(self):
        print("Playing radio")

car = Car()
car.start()   # Output: Starting vehicle\nStarting car engine
car.play_radio()   # Output: Playing radio
car.stop()   # Output: Stopping vehicle\nStopping car engine
```

2. Shape, Square, and Circle classes:

```python
class Shape:
    def area(self):
        pass

class Square(Shape):
    def __init__(self, side_length):
        self.side_length = side_length

    def area(self):
        return self.side_length ** 2

class Circle(Shape):
    def __init__(self, radius):
        self.radius = radius

    def area(self):
        return 3.14159 * (self.radius ** 2)

square = Square(4)
print(square.area())   # Output: 16

circle = Circle(3)
```

```
print(circle.area())   # Output: 28.27331
```

Feel ready to take inheritance head-on now? Awesome, let's keep the momentum going!

Multiple Inheritance: Mastering Complexity

Introduction
Multiple inheritance is a feature that allows a class to inherit attributes and methods from more than one parent class. While this gives you significant power and flexibility, it also introduces a layer of complexity that needs careful management. Ready? Let's go!

Learning Objectives
- Understand what multiple inheritance is.
- Learn how to implement multiple inheritance in Python.
- Get acquainted with Python's method resolution order (MRO).

The Basics of Multiple Inheritance
In Python, a class can inherit from multiple parent classes, making it a true multi-paradigm language. However, this feature should be used judiciously. Here's a simple example:

```python
# Example: Multiple Inheritance
class Parent1:
    def show(self):
        print("This is Parent1.")

class Parent2:
    def display(self):
        print("This is Parent2.")

class Child(Parent1, Parent2):
    pass

obj = Child()
obj.show()      # Output: This is Parent1.
obj.display()   # Output: This is Parent2.
```

In this example, the `Child` class inherits from both `Parent1` and `Parent2`.

Method Resolution Order (MRO)

When using multiple inheritance, Python uses a technique called Method Resolution Order (MRO) to determine the sequence in which base classes are searched when looking for a method. The algorithm used for this is called C3 Linearization.

You can examine the MRO of a class using the .__mro__ attribute or the mro() method.

```
# Example: Checking MRO
print(Child.mro())
```

Overriding and Extending in Multiple Inheritance

You can also override or extend methods in multiple inheritance, similar to single inheritance.

```
# Example: Overriding in Multiple Inheritance
class Parent1:
    def show(self):
        print("This is Parent1.")

class Parent2:
    def show(self):
        print("This is Parent2.")

class Child(Parent1, Parent2):
    def show(self):
        super().show()
        print("This is Child.")

obj = Child()
obj.show()
# Output: This is Parent1.
#         This is Child.
```

In this example, `Child` overrides the `show()` method but also uses `super()` to call `Parent1`'s `show()` method.

Exercises

1. Create a `Mammal` class and a `Bird` class with different methods. Create a `Bat` class that inherits from both and overrides a method.
2. Implement a `Polygon` class and then implement `Triangle` and `Rectangle` classes. Create a `Square` class that inherits from both `Triangle` and `Rectangle`.

Best Practices

- Use multiple inheritance cautiously; it can lead to a complicated and tangled class hierarchy.
- Always check the MRO if you're dealing with multiple inheritance.
- Consider using Mixins for more straightforward code sharing.

Solutions to the Exercises

1. Mammal, Bird, and Bat classes:

```python
class Mammal:
    def sound(self):
        print("Mammal sound")

class Bird:
    def sound(self):
        print("Bird sound")

class Bat(Mammal, Bird):
    def sound(self):
        super().sound()
        print("Bat sound")

bat = Bat()
bat.sound()
# Output: Mammal sound
#         Bat sound
```

2. Polygon, Triangle, Rectangle, and Square classes:

```python
class Polygon:
    def sides(self):
        pass

class Triangle(Polygon):
    def sides(self):
        return 3

class Rectangle(Polygon):
    def sides(self):
        return 4

class Square(Triangle, Rectangle):
    def sides(self):
        return super().sides()

square = Square()
print(square.sides())   # Output: 3
```

Now you're equipped to make the most of multiple inheritance in Python! What's next on our programming journey? Stay tuned to find out!

Deep Dive on Polymorphism: One Interface, Many Implementations

Introduction

Polymorphism is one of the four pillars of Object-Oriented Programming (OOP). The term comes from the Greek words "Poly" (many) and "Morph" (forms), and in the context of programming, it allows us to use a single interface to represent different types. It's like having a universal remote that can control a TV, an air conditioner, and a music system. So, let's jump in and explore how Python offers multiple avenues for implementing polymorphism.

Learning Objectives

- Grasp what polymorphism is and why it's useful.
- Understand the different ways to achieve polymorphism in Python.
- Learn about the role of duck typing in Python's polymorphism.

The Essence of Polymorphism

In Python, polymorphism allows us to define methods in the child class with the same name as defined in their parent class. Let's look at an example to get started:

```python
class Animal:
    def make_sound(self):
        return "Some generic sound"

class Dog(Animal):
    def make_sound(self):
        return "Woof"

class Cat(Animal):
    def make_sound(self):
        return "Meow"

def animal_sound(animal):
    print(animal.make_sound())

# Test our polymorphism
animal_sound(Dog())    # Output: Woof
animal_sound(Cat())    # Output: Meow
```

Here, the function `animal_sound` doesn't need to know the type of animal to call the `make_sound` method. That's polymorphism in action!

113

Function Overloading

Python doesn't support traditional function overloading where you can define the same method multiple times with different parameters. However, you can achieve a similar result using default arguments or variable-length arguments.

```python
# Example: Function overloading using default arguments
def add(a, b=0, c=0):
    return a + b + c

print(add(1))       # Output: 1
print(add(1, 2))    # Output: 3
print(add(1, 2, 3))# Output: 6
```

Operator Overloading

Python allows us to overload operators, which is another form of polymorphism. You can redefine the meaning of operators for custom objects.

```python
class ComplexNumber:
    def __init__(self, r, i):
        self.real = r
        self.imag = i

    def __add__(self, other):
        return ComplexNumber(self.real + other.real, self.imag + other.imag)

# Example
num1 = ComplexNumber(2, 3)
num2 = ComplexNumber(1, 2)
result = num1 + num2
```

Duck Typing: Python's Unique Flair

In Python, you don't need to explicitly specify types, thanks to dynamic typing, a feature affectionately known as duck typing. The principle behind duck typing is simple: "If it looks like a duck, swims like a duck, and quacks like a duck, then it probably is a duck."

Exercises

1. Create a `Shape` class with a method `area`. Create `Square` and `Circle` classes and override the `area` method. Use polymorphism to find the area for both shapes.
2. Create a `calculate` function that can accept both integers and lists. If it's an integer, square it; if it's a list, sum it.

Best Practices

- Use polymorphism judiciously; it makes code more extendable and maintainable but can introduce complexity.
- Always comment your code well, especially when using operator overloading and duck typing, as these features could make the code less readable for others.

Solutions to the Exercises

1. `Shape`, `Square`, and `Circle` classes:

```python
class Shape:
    def area(self):
        pass

class Square(Shape):
    def __init__(self, side):
        self.side = side

    def area(self):
        return self.side ** 2

class Circle(Shape):
    def __init__(self, radius):
        self.radius = radius

    def area(self):
        return 3.14159 * self.radius ** 2

def find_area(shape):
    print(shape.area())

# Test
find_area(Square(4))    # Output: 16
find_area(Circle(3))    # Output: 28.27331
```

2. `calculate` function:

```python
def calculate(value):
    if isinstance(value, int):
        return value ** 2
    elif isinstance(value, list):
        return sum(value)
```

```
# Test
print(calculate(4))         # Output: 16
print(calculate([1, 2, 3])) # Output: 6
```

Polymorphism and Method Overriding: Customizing Object Behavior

The method overriding lets you change the behavior of methods in a derived class, letting you tailor each object's capabilities. Let's dive in!

Learning Objectives

- Understand what method overriding is and its relationship with polymorphism.
- Recognize when and why to use method overriding.
- Learn about the use of the super() function.

What Is Method Overriding?

Method overriding is a feature that enables a subclass to provide its own version of a method that is already defined in its superclass. The overriden method in the subclass must have the same name, signature, and parameters as the method in the superclass.

```
class Animal:
    def make_sound(self):
        return "Some generic sound"

class Dog(Animal):
    def make_sound(self):
        return "Woof"

# Now Dog class overrides the make_sound method from Animal class
dog = Dog()
print(dog.make_sound())   # Output: Woof
```

When to Use Method Overriding?

Method overriding is generally used for one of the following reasons:

- To provide a specific implementation of a method that is already provided by its superclass.
- To improve upon or extend the functionality of an existing method from the superclass.

The super() Function: Accessing Parent Powers

Sometimes you might want to call the overridden method from the parent class within the child class. You can do this using super().

116

```
class Cat(Animal):
    def make_sound(self):
        original_sound = super().make_sound()
        return f"Cat says {original_sound} but prefers to Meow."

cat = Cat()
print(cat.make_sound())    # Output: Cat says Some generic sound but prefers to Meow.
```

Best Practices

- Use method overriding only when it's genuinely necessary. Unnecessary overriding can make the code more complex and harder to maintain.
- Be cautious about using `super()` as it can make the method dependent on the parent class's implementation, reducing flexibility.

Exercises

1. Create a `Vehicle` class with a method `fuel_efficiency()`. Override this method in derived classes like `Car` and `Bike`.

2. Extend the `Animal` class to include other animals like `Fish` and `Bird`. Override the `make_sound` method for each.

Solutions to the Exercises

1. `Vehicle`, `Car`, and `Bike` classes

```
class Vehicle:
    def fuel_efficiency(self):
        return "This vehicle's fuel efficiency is unknown."

class Car(Vehicle):
    def fuel_efficiency(self):
        return "This car's fuel efficiency is 25 MPG."

class Bike(Vehicle):
    def fuel_efficiency(self):
        return "This bike does not consume fuel."

# Test
car = Car()
bike = Bike()
print(car.fuel_efficiency())   # Output: This car's fuel efficiency is 25 MPG.
print(bike.fuel_efficiency())  # Output: This bike does not consume fuel.
```

2. Extending `Animal` class:

117

```
class Fish(Animal):
    def make_sound(self):
        return "Blub"

class Bird(Animal):
    def make_sound(self):
        return "Tweet"

# Test
fish = Fish()
bird = Bird()
print(fish.make_sound())   # Output: Blub
print(bird.make_sound())   # Output: Tweet
```

Go ahead, customize your objects and make them as unique as they can be. Happy coding!

The Base Class: The Unsung Hero of Object-Oriented Programming

What Is a Base Class?

A base class, often known as a parent or superclass, serves as the foundational blueprint for other classes, known as derived, child, or subclass. The base class outlines common attributes and behaviors that can be shared across its subclasses.

```
# A simple example
class Shape:
    def area(self):
        pass

    def perimeter(self):
        pass
```

Here, Shape would be the base class, while specific shapes like Square, Triangle, and Circle would be the subclasses.

Why Do We Need a Base Class?

1. Reusability: The base class defines common methods that can be overridden or extended by subclasses.

2. Maintainability: Modifications in the base class propagate to all its subclasses, making maintenance easier.

2. Polymorphism: With a well-defined base class, you can manipulate multiple object types (the subclasses) through a unified interface.

Defining a Base Class Effectively

A good base class should:
- Be abstract enough to cover all the basic functionalities required by the subclasses.
- Not be overly restrictive, allowing enough flexibility for subclasses to extend or customize these functionalities.

The super() Function: Your Direct Line to the Base Class

The super() function lets you call a method from a parent class inside a derived class. It's your direct line to the base class when you need to access its attributes or methods.

```python
class Rectangle(Shape):
    def __init__(self, length, width):
        self.length = length
        self.width = width

    def area(self):
        return self.length * self.width

    def perimeter(self):
        return 2 * (self.length + self.width)

class Square(Rectangle):
    def __init__(self, side):
        super().__init__(side, side)
```

Best Practices
- Make sure the base class has well-documented methods to guide the developers who are extending it.
- Do not put too much logic into the base class; it's a blueprint, not a catch-all solution.

Exercises

1. Define a base class Vehicle and subclasses Car and Boat. Implement methods like move() in both.
2. Extend the base class Shape to create subclasses for Triangle and Hexagon.

Solutions to the Exercises

1. Vehicle, Car, and Boat classes:

```python
class Vehicle:
    def move(self):
        print("This vehicle moves.")
```

```
class Car(Vehicle):
    def move(self):
        print("This car drives on roads.")

class Boat(Vehicle):
    def move(self):
        print("This boat sails on water.")

# Test
car = Car()
boat = Boat()
car.move()   # Output: This car drives on roads.
boat.move()  # Output: This boat sails on water.
```

2. Extending Shape class:

```
class Triangle(Shape):
    def area(self):
        # Implement area calculation for a triangle
        pass

    def perimeter(self):
        # Implement perimeter calculation for a triangle
        pass

class Hexagon(Shape):
    def area(self):
        # Implement area calculation for a hexagon
        pass

    def perimeter(self):
        # Implement perimeter calculation for a hexagon
        pass
```

Encapsulation (Hiding Object's Attributes)

Let's talk about one of the most intriguing but crucial concepts in Object-Oriented Programming (OOP) – encapsulation. Specifically, we'll focus on how to hide an object's attributes, keeping them safe from unnecessary external interference. Yes, it's like putting your precious belongings in a safe!

Learning Objectives

- Understand the concept of encapsulation in OOP
- Learn the importance of hiding object attributes
- Grasp different ways to achieve encapsulation in Python

The Importance of Hiding Object Attributes

Imagine your bank details were available to anyone who asked. Scary, right? Similarly, you don't want every part of your code to have access to specific object attributes. That's where encapsulation comes in handy. It restricts access to certain details of an object and prevents unauthorized modifications.

Information Overload

One common pitfall in programming is information overload. When attributes are all over the place, the complexity increases, and mistakes are bound to happen. Hiding attributes helps in reducing complexity by narrowing down the points of interaction.

Enhancing Flexibility

What if you want to change how an attribute works in the future? If it's exposed and used in many places, making that change is like walking through a minefield. But if it's hidden and accessed via methods, you can safely change it without affecting the rest of the codebase.

Achieving Encapsulation in Python

The Underscore Game: _ and __

In Python, you'll often see attributes prefixed with underscores. This is not just a naming convention but a way to indicate the visibility of attributes.

- **Single Underscore**: `_attribute`
  This is a weak "internal use" indicator. It tells the programmer to be cautious, but it won't prevent access.
- **Double Underscore**: `__attribute`
  This changes the attribute name to include the class name (`_ClassName__attribute`). This makes it harder (but not impossible) to access the attribute externally.

Here's a quick example:

```python
class BankAccount:
    def __init__(self):
        self._balance = 0        # weak internal use
        self.__pin = 1234        # attribute name mangling

    def deposit(self, amount):
        self._balance += amount

    def get_balance(self):
```

```
        return self._balance
```

Property Decorators: *@property* and *@attribute.setter*

Python provides @property and @attribute.setter decorators to define methods for getting and setting attribute values, effectively hiding the actual attribute.

```python
class BankAccount:
    def __init__(self):
        self._balance = 0

    @property
    def balance(self):
        return self._balance

    @balance.setter
    def balance(self, amount):
        if amount >= 0:
            self._balance = amount
```

Exercises

1. Create a class Person with a private attribute __age. Use a method to set the age only if it is greater than or equal to 0.
2. Extend the BankAccount class to include a method that sets the pin. Make the pin private.
3. Implement a Car class with a private __speed attribute. Include methods to accelerate and brake, ensuring the speed never falls below 0.

Solutions to the Exercises

Exercise 1

```python
class Person:
    def __init__(self, age=0):
        self.__age = None
        self.set_age(age)

    def set_age(self, age):
        if age >= 0:
            self.__age = age
```

Exercise 2

```python
class BankAccount:
    def __init__(self, pin):
```

```
        self.__pin = pin

    def set_pin(self, new_pin):
        self.__pin = new_pin
```

Exercise 3

```
class Car:
    def __init__(self):
        self.__speed = 0

    def accelerate(self):
        self.__speed += 5

    def brake(self):
        self.__speed = max(0, self.__speed - 5)
```

Keep these principles in mind, and you'll be writing solid, maintainable code in no time.

_Deep Dive on Abstraction: Simplifying Complexity in Object-Oriented Programming

In simple terms, abstraction means showing only what's necessary and hiding the underlying complexity. In OOP, abstraction lets you present a simplified interface for more complex operations.

Why Abstraction?

1. Simplicity: Abstraction lets developers interact with objects without needing to understand the inner workings fully.
2. Maintainability: You can change the underlying code without affecting the areas of the program that interact with the abstracted part.
3. Extensibility: An abstract class can serve as a foundation for multiple subclasses, making it easier to add new features.

Implementing Abstraction in Python

Python provides abstract classes through the ABC (Abstract Base Classes) module. An abstract class can define abstract methods that must be implemented by any subclass.

Here's a simple example:

```
from abc import ABC, abstractmethod

class Shape(ABC):

    @abstractmethod
    def area(self):
```

```
        pass

    @abstractmethod
    def perimeter(self):
        pass
```

In this example, Shape is an abstract class with two abstract methods: area() and perimeter().

Making It Concrete: Subclasses and Abstraction

The power of abstraction becomes clear when you create subclasses:

```
class Rectangle(Shape):
    def __init__(self, length, width):
        self.length = length
        self.width = width

    def area(self):
        return self.length * self.width

    def perimeter(self):
        return 2 * (self.length + self.width)
```

Exercise:

Create an abstract class called Animal with methods speak and eat. Create subclasses Dog and Cat that implement these methods.

Solution to Exercise

1. Animal, Dog, and Cat classes:

```
from abc import ABC, abstractmethod

class Animal(ABC):
    @abstractmethod
    def speak(self):
        pass

    @abstractmethod
    def eat(self):
        pass

class Dog(Animal):
    def speak(self):
        return "Woof!"
```

```
    def eat(self):
        return "Eating dog food"

class Cat(Animal):
    def speak(self):
        return "Meow!"

    def eat(self):
        return "Eating cat food"
```
To test it:
```
dog = Dog()
cat = Cat()


print(dog.speak())    # Output: Woof!
print(cat.eat())      # Output: Eating cat food
```

_ *Operator Overloading in Python*

Operator overloading, sometimes called "operator ad-hoc polymorphism," is a way to define how operators work for user-defined objects. In Python, this is achieved using special methods, often referred to as "magic" or "dunder" methods, which stand for "double underscore" methods like __add__, __sub__, __mul__, etc.

Why Operator Overloading?

Imagine you've created a `Vector` class to represent 2D vectors. Wouldn't it be nice to add two vectors using the + operator, like you do with integers or floats? That's precisely where operator overloading comes into play. By defining a method like __add__ in your class, you can control what the + operator does.

The Magic Methods

Let's have a look at some commonly used magic methods you can define to overload operators.

- __add__: Addition (+)
- __sub__: Subtraction (−)
- __mul__: Multiplication (*)
- __truediv__: Division (/)
- __floordiv__: Floor Division (//)
- __mod__: Modulus (%)
- __pow__: Power (**)

Here's a simplistic example to demonstrate how to implement these:

```
class ComplexNumber:
    def __init__(self, real, imag):
```

```
        self.real = real
        self.imag = imag

    def __add__(self, other):
        return ComplexNumber(self.real + other.real, self.imag + other.imag)

    def __sub__(self, other):
        return ComplexNumber(self.real - other.real, self.imag - other.imag)

    # You can define other magic methods similarly.

    def __str__(self):
        return f"{self.real} + {self.imag}i"
```

A Few Caveats

1. Consistency: Your overloaded operator should make sense. If + is addition for a mathematical object, it shouldn't become subtraction suddenly in your implementation.
2. Don't Go Overboard: Overloading every operator could make your code confusing and hard to debug. Stick to the ones that genuinely add clarity and functionality.

When to Use

- Mathematical Models: Overload operators to implement mathematical operations cleanly.
- String Representation: For custom string formats, you can overload __str__ and __repr__.

Exercises

1. Create a Vector class and implement __add__ and __sub__ methods to add and subtract vectors.
2. Implement a Fraction class that overloads __mul__ and __truediv__ to multiply and divide fractions.

Solutions to the Exercises

Exercise 1: Vector Class

Here's how you can implement a Vector class that supports vector addition and subtraction using the __add__ and __sub__ methods.

```
class Vector:
    def __init__(self, x, y):
        self.x = x
        self.y = y

    def __add__(self, other):
        return Vector(self.x + other.x, self.y + other.y)
```

```python
    def __sub__(self, other):
        return Vector(self.x - other.x, self.y - other.y)

    def __str__(self):
        return f"Vector({self.x}, {self.y})"

# Test the Vector class
v1 = Vector(2, 3)
v2 = Vector(1, 1)

# Add vectors
result_add = v1 + v2
print(f"The result of addition is: {result_add}")

# Subtract vectors
result_sub = v1 - v2
print(f"The result of subtraction is: {result_sub}")
```

When you run this code, it should output:

```csharp
csharpCopy code
The result of addition is: Vector(3, 4)
The result of subtraction is: Vector(1, 2)
```

Exercise 2: Fraction Class

For the `Fraction` class, you can overload the `__mul__` and `__truediv__` methods as follows:

```python
from math import gcd

class Fraction:
    def __init__(self, numerator, denominator):
        self.numerator = numerator
        self.denominator = denominator

    def simplify(self):
        common_gcd = gcd(self.numerator, self.denominator)
        self.numerator //= common_gcd
        self.denominator //= common_gcd

    def __mul__(self, other):
        new_numerator = self.numerator * other.numerator
        new_denominator = self.denominator * other.denominator
        result = Fraction(new_numerator, new_denominator)
```

```python
        result.simplify()
        return result

    def __truediv__(self, other):
        new_numerator = self.numerator * other.denominator
        new_denominator = self.denominator * other.numerator
        result = Fraction(new_numerator, new_denominator)
        result.simplify()
        return result

    def __str__(self):
        return f"{self.numerator}/{self.denominator}"

# Test the Fraction class
f1 = Fraction(2, 3)
f2 = Fraction(3, 4)

# Multiply fractions
result_mul = f1 * f2
print(f"The result of multiplication is: {result_mul}")

# Divide fractions
result_div = f1 / f2
print(f"The result of division is: {result_div}")
```

When you run this code, it should output:

```csharp
csharpCopy code
The result of multiplication is: 1/2
The result of division is: 8/9
```

I hope these solutions clarify how to implement operator overloading for custom classes in Python!

Chapter 12: Python Libraries and Frameworks

Intro

The beauty of Python lies not just in its syntax or community support, but also in its extensive collection of libraries and frameworks that make your life easier. Trust me, there's a reason Python has been crowned the Swiss Army Knife of programming languages.

What Are Libraries and Frameworks?

A **library** is essentially a pre-written piece of code that you can call upon to solve common problems. Think of it as a toolbox you can reach into when you need a screwdriver or a wrench.

On the other hand, a **framework** is like an empty house where the walls, roof, and foundation are already built. You just need to furnish it according to your needs. Frameworks usually have a more opinionated structure, and they provide a scaffold that helps you build applications more efficiently.

Why Are They So Important?

1. Time-Saving: Libraries and frameworks drastically reduce the time you need to bring an application to market. No need to reinvent the wheel when someone has already built it for you!

2. Optimized Performance: The pre-written code in libraries and frameworks is often optimized and tested by a community of experts, which makes it more efficient and secure.

3. Community Support: If you're using a popular library or framework, chances are you'll find an active community of developers who are willing to help out with issues and questions.

4. Compatibility & Scalability: Many libraries and frameworks are designed to be compatible with other technologies and to scale easily, thus making your life easier when your project grows.

Types of Libraries

1. Standard Libraries: Python comes packed with a rich standard library that caters to a broad array of tasks. These include libraries for file I/O, regular expressions, and even web development (yes, you heard it right).

2. Third-Party Libraries: These are libraries developed by the Python community and are not bundled with Python. The famous `pip` is your friend here, helping you install these additional tools.

Types of Frameworks

1. Web Frameworks: Django and Flask are the stars here, assisting you in web development tasks, from routing to templating and database management.

2. Scientific Frameworks: Libraries like TensorFlow and PyTorch fall into this category, assisting in machine learning and scientific computation.

3. Game Development Frameworks: Pygame is a great example that helps you craft video games with Python.

The Must-Know Libraries and Frameworks

1. NumPy: This one's a lifesaver when it comes to numerical computations.

2. Pandas: Data wrangling and data frames? Pandas is your go-to library.

3. Matplotlib: For all your data visualization needs.

4. Django: A high-level framework that encourages clean, practical design.

5. Flask: A micro-framework that's more flexible than Django but requires more setup.

6. TensorFlow and PyTorch: The pillars of machine learning and artificial intelligence.

Wrapping Up

Look, when it comes to Python, learning the language is just the tip of the iceberg. Knowing which library or framework to use for what is like having a roadmap that guides you through this endless universe of possibilities.

Exercises

1. Exercise 1: Research and find a Python library or framework that interests you which hasn't been covered above. Write a brief summary explaining what it does.
2. Exercise 2: Install any third-party library using `pip` and write a simple program that uses it.

Numpy and Scientific Computing

NumPy is a library that serves as the backbone of scientific computing in Python. If numbers make you tick, then NumPy will make your heart race. Sounds dramatic? Well, read on!

The Magic Called NumPy

So, what's the buzz around NumPy? Short for 'Numerical Python,' NumPy is a Python library used for working with arrays. Wait, Python has lists, so why arrays? Well, arrays are way more efficient and provide a host of built-in functions to make your life easier. Plus, they play nicely with other libraries like Pandas and Matplotlib.

Why NumPy for Scientific Computing?

1. Speed: Ever heard of 'C'? No, not the ocean! I'm talking about the programming language. NumPy is written in C, which makes it insanely fast.
2. Memory Efficiency: NumPy arrays are more memory-efficient than lists. They allow you to store more data in less space, so it's a win-win!
3. Mathematical Functions: From basic (like add, subtract) to advanced operations (like Fourier Transform), NumPy has got it all.
4. Interoperability: NumPy can seamlessly interface with libraries written in C, C++, or Fortran, making it a versatile choice for scientific computations.

Installing NumPy

Getting NumPy on your machine is a breeze. Open up your terminal and type:

```
pip install numpy
```

Voila! You've got NumPy installed.

The Core: NumPy Arrays

At the heart of NumPy are arrays. Let's look at different types of arrays you can create:

1. One-Dimensional Array: It's the simplest form of array that enables you to organize a series of items sequentially.

```
import numpy as np
arr = np.array([1, 2, 3])
```

2. Multi-Dimensional Array: Think of it as an array of arrays.

```
multi_arr = np.array([[1, 2], [3, 4], [5, 6]])
```

Slicing and Dicing Arrays

NumPy arrays support slicing. You can grab a portion of an array using slice notation, which is quite similar to Python lists.

```
arr = np.array([1, 2, 3, 4, 5])
first_two_elements = arr[0:2]
```

Mathematical Operations

What's science without some math, right? NumPy offers a plethora of mathematical functions.

1. Arithmetic Operations: Add, subtract, multiply, and divide arrays element-wise.

```
np.add(arr1, arr2)
np.subtract(arr1, arr2)
```

2. Statistical Operations: Functions like `mean`, `median`, `max`, and `min` come in handy for statistical analysis.

3. Matrix Operations: Matrix multiplication, transposition, and determinants are just a method call away.

4. Fourier Transform and More: Advanced operations like Fourier Transform can be performed seamlessly.

Advanced Features

1. Broadcasting: NumPy allows you to perform arithmetic operations on arrays of different shapes and sizes.
2. Masking: If you want to extract specific elements based on a condition, masking is your tool.
3. Stacking: Combine multiple arrays either vertically (vstack) or horizontally (hstack).

Some Tips and Tricks

1. Use np.linspace(start, end, num) to create an array with evenly spaced num numbers between start and end.
2. For large datasets, consider using NumPy's memmap to read a large array from disk without loading it entirely into memory.
3. The np.where() function is great for replacing elements in an array based on a condition.

Exercises

Exercise 1: Create a two-dimensional NumPy array and perform matrix multiplication.
Exercise 2: Use NumPy's statistical functions to analyze a dataset of your choice.

Exercise 3: Use NumPy to perform Fourier Transform on a simple data set.

Certainly, let's get down to solving those exercises.

Solutions to the Exercises

Exercise 1: Create a two-dimensional NumPy array and perform matrix multiplication.

```
import numpy as np

# Create two 2D arrays (matrices)
matrix1 = np.array([[1, 2], [3, 4]])
matrix2 = np.array([[5, 6], [7, 8]])

# Perform matrix multiplication using np.dot() function
result_matrix = np.dot(matrix1, matrix2)
print("Result of matrix multiplication: \n", result_matrix)
When you run this code, you should get:
luaCopy code
Result of matrix multiplication:
[[19 22]
 [43 50]]
```

Exercise 2: Use NumPy's statistical functions to analyze a dataset of your choice.

Let's say we have a dataset of test scores for 10 students.

```
test_scores = np.array([89, 90, 78, 92, 88, 76, 93, 85, 86, 94])

# Calculate mean, median, max, and min scores
mean_score = np.mean(test_scores)
median_score = np.median(test_scores)
max_score = np.max(test_scores)
min_score = np.min(test_scores)

print(f"Mean Score: {mean_score}")
print(f"Median Score: {median_score}")
print(f"Max Score: {max_score}")
print(f"Min Score: {min_score}")
Output will be:
mathematicaCopy code
Mean Score: 87.1
Median Score: 88.0
```

```
Max Score: 94
Min Score: 76
```

Exercise 3: Use NumPy to perform Fourier Transform on a simple data set.

For this exercise, let's consider a simple sine wave.

```python
import matplotlib.pyplot as plt

# Create a sine wave
t = np.linspace(0, 1, 500, endpoint=False)
y = np.sin(2 * np.pi * 7 * t)

# Perform Fourier Transform
y_fft = np.fft.fft(y)

# Plot the real part of Fourier Transform
plt.plot(np.real(y_fft))
plt.show()
```

This code will plot the real part of the Fourier Transform of a sine wave. You can also examine the imaginary part by replacing `np.real(y_fft)` with `np.imag(y_fft)`.

We've solved the exercises and hopefully added some clarity to the versatile world of NumPy. Keep practicing, and don't hesitate to get your hands dirty with more complex datasets and operations. Happy Computing!

_Data Manipulation with Pandas: Your Swiss Army Knife for Data

Ah, Pandas! If data manipulation is an art, then Pandas is your paintbrush. Named after "Panel Data," and not the adorable bear, this library has gained its place as a cornerstone in the Python data science ecosystem. Let's dive in and explore what makes Pandas such a crucial tool.

What Is Pandas?

Pandas is a Python library built on top of NumPy, aiming to provide rich, easy-to-use data structures and methods to manipulate and analyze structured data. With Pandas, you can handle a plethora of data types—ranging from simple datasets to multi-dimensional time-series data. The two main components are Series and DataFrame.

- **Series**: A one-dimensional array capable of holding any data type. Think of it like a column in a spreadsheet.
- **DataFrame**: A two-dimensional tabular data structure, sort of like a spreadsheet, database table, or a dictionary of Series.

Installing Pandas

Before diving deep into functionalities, let's ensure Pandas is on your system. If not, install it with a simple pip command:

```
pip install pandas
```

Creating a DataFrame

Once installed, creating a DataFrame is as simple as this:

```python
import pandas as pd

data = {'Name': ['Alice', 'Bob', 'Carol'],
        'Age': [25, 30, 35],
        'Occupation': ['Engineer', 'Doctor', 'Artist']}

df = pd.DataFrame(data)
```

Importing and Exporting Data

To read data from a CSV file:

```python
df = pd.read_csv('data.csv')
```

And to write it back to a CSV:

```python
df.to_csv('new_data.csv', index=False)
```

Pandas supports many more formats like JSON, Excel, and SQL databases.

Basic Data Exploration

Data loaded? Great! Let's explore:

```python
# Show the first 5 rows
df.head()

# Show basic statistics
df.describe()
```

Indexing and Selection

Select a specific column:

```python
age = df['Age']
```

Or multiple columns:

```python
subset = df[['Name', 'Occupation']]
```

Data Filtering

You can also filter data based on conditions:

```
filtered_data = df[df['Age'] > 30]
```

Handling Missing Data

Pandas has robust ways to deal with missing data:

```
# Drop rows with missing values
df.dropna()


# Fill missing values with zero
df.fillna(0)
```

Data Transformation and Aggregation

You can apply functions to DataFrame columns or rows:

```
# Using a lambda function to square ages
df['Age'] = df['Age'].apply(lambda x: x**2)


# Using built-in aggregation functions
df['Age'].sum()
```

Merging and Joining DataFrames

Combining data in Pandas is simple:

```
merged_df = pd.merge(df1, df2, on='ID')
```

Time Series Manipulation

Pandas also excels in time-series data manipulation, from simple date-range creation to shifting and resampling time-series data.

Exercises

1. Create a DataFrame from a list and dictionary and explore the basic statistics.
2. Read a CSV File and filter out rows based on a condition.
3. Handle Missing Data: Use dropna() and fillna() to manage missing data in your DataFrame.
4. Aggregate Data: Use Pandas aggregation functions like mean() and sum() on your DataFrame.

Solutions to the Exercises on Data Manipulation with Pandas

Exercise 1: Create a DataFrame

The first exercise requires you to create a DataFrame from a list and dictionary and then explore its basic statistics.

```
import pandas as pd

# Create DataFrame from Dictionary
data_dict = {'Name': ['John', 'Jane', 'Jack'], 'Age': [25, 30, 35]}
df_dict = pd.DataFrame(data_dict)

# Create DataFrame from List
data_list = [['Amy', 40], ['Bob', 45], ['Carl', 50]]
df_list = pd.DataFrame(data_list, columns=['Name', 'Age'])

# Basic Statistics
print(df_dict.describe())
print(df_list.describe())
```

Exercise 2: Read a CSV File

For this exercise, you would have to read a CSV file and then filter out rows based on a condition. We'll assume the CSV file has a column named 'Age'.

```
# Read CSV file into DataFrame
df = pd.read_csv('sample.csv')

# Filter out rows where 'Age' is greater than 30
filtered_df = df[df['Age'] > 30]
```

Exercise 3: Handle Missing Data

This exercise asks you to handle missing data in your DataFrame using the dropna() and fillna() methods.

```
# Sample DataFrame with Missing Data
data = {'Name': ['Anna', None, 'Charles'], 'Age': [20, None, 30]}
df_missing = pd.DataFrame(data)

# Drop rows with missing values
df_dropped = df_missing.dropna()

# Fill missing values with 0
df_filled = df_missing.fillna(0)
```

Exercise 4: Aggregate Data

The last exercise is about aggregating data in your DataFrame using Pandas built-in aggregation functions.

```
# Sample DataFrame
data = {'Salary': [40000, 50000, 60000]}
df_salary = pd.DataFrame(data)

# Calculate Mean Salary
mean_salary = df_salary['Salary'].mean()

# Calculate Sum of Salary
sum_salary = df_salary['Salary'].sum()
```

Visualizing Data with Matplotlib: A Comprehensive Guide

Visualizing your allows you to understand the data's trends, patterns, and insights, which are otherwise difficult to glean from raw data. One of the most powerful libraries for data visualization in Python is Matplotlib. So, let's dive into the magical world of Matplotlib and make our data speak.

What is Matplotlib?

Matplotlib is a Python library designed for data plotting and visualization. It provides a wide variety of plots like line charts, bar graphs, scatter plots, and much more. It's like the Swiss Army knife of data visualization in Python.

Installation and Importing

Before anything else, you have to install Matplotlib. You can easily do this using pip:

```
pip install matplotlib
```

Once installed, you can import it into your Python script.

```
import matplotlib.pyplot as plt
```

Basic Plotting

Creating a basic plot is as simple as calling a single function.

```
# Data
x = [1, 2, 3, 4]
y = [1, 4, 9, 16]

# Create Plot
plt.plot(x, y)
plt.show()
```

The `plt.plot()` function plots the data points and connects them with lines. The `plt.show()` function displays the plot.

Adding Titles and Labels

A plot without titles and labels is like a book without a cover. Here's how to add them:

```
plt.plot(x, y)
plt.title('Basic Plot')
plt.xlabel('x-axis')
plt.ylabel('y-axis')
plt.show()
```

Multiple Plots

You can create multiple plots in a single chart using the `subplot` function. For example:

```
plt.subplot(1, 2, 1) # 1 row, 2 columns, first plot
plt.plot(x, y)
plt.title('First Plot')

plt.subplot(1, 2, 2) # 1 row, 2 columns, second plot
plt.plot(y, x)
plt.title('Second Plot')

plt.show()
```

Types of Plots

Matplotlib isn't limited to line plots. You can also create:
- Bar Graphs
- Histograms
- Scatter Plots
- Pie Charts
- And more!

Here's a quick example of a bar graph:

```
labels = ['Apple', 'Banana', 'Cherry']
values = [5, 7, 3]

plt.bar(labels, values)
plt.show()
```

Customization

Matplotlib allows a wide range of customization. For example, you can change the color, marker style, line style, etc.

```
plt.plot(x, y, color='red', marker='o', linestyle='--')
```

```
plt.show()
```

Plotting with NumPy Arrays

NumPy arrays can be directly used in Matplotlib functions.

```
import numpy as np

x = np.linspace(0, 10, 100)
y = np.sin(x)

plt.plot(x, y)
plt.show()
```

Visualizing DataFrames with Pandas and Matplotlib

Combining Pandas and Matplotlib allows for efficient data manipulation and visualization.

```
import pandas as pd

data = {'x_values': [1, 2, 3], 'y_values': [1, 4, 9]}
df = pd.DataFrame(data)

plt.plot('x_values', 'y_values', data=df)
plt.show()
```

Error Bars

Error bars provide an additional layer of information on data variability.

```
plt.errorbar(x, y, yerr=0.2, fmt='o')
plt.show()
```

Saving Plots

You can easily save your plots in various formats.

```
plt.savefig('plot.png')
```

Exercises

1. Create a line plot for the equation $y=x2y = x^2y=x2$ for x ranging from -10 to 10.
2. Create a bar graph representing the sales of a retail store for the year 2022, with data for each month.
3. Create a scatter plot with random points and add a line of best fit.
4. Generate a histogram using random data.

Solutions to the Exercises

Exercise 1: Create a line plot for the equation y=x2y = x^2y=x2 for x ranging from -10 to 10.

```python
import matplotlib.pyplot as plt
import numpy as np

# Create an array of x values from -10 to 10
x = np.linspace(-10, 10, 100)
y = x ** 2

plt.plot(x, y)
plt.title("Plot of \( y = x^2 \)")
plt.xlabel("x")
plt.ylabel("y")
plt.show()
```

Exercise 2: Create a bar graph representing the sales of a retail store for the year 2022, with data for each month.

```python
months = ['Jan', 'Feb', 'Mar', 'Apr', 'May', 'Jun', 'Jul', 'Aug', 'Sep', 'Oct', 'Nov',
'Dec']
sales = [200, 220, 250, 275, 300, 320, 350, 370, 400, 420, 450, 480]

plt.bar(months, sales)
plt.title('Sales Data for 2022')
plt.xlabel('Months')
plt.ylabel('Sales in $')
plt.show()
```

Exercise 3: Create a scatter plot with random points and add a line of best fit.

```python
import numpy as np
import matplotlib.pyplot as plt

# Generate random points
x = np.random.rand(50)
y = 2 * x + 1 + np.random.randn(50) * 0.5

# Line of best fit
coefficients = np.polyfit(x, y, 1)
polynomial = np.poly1d(coefficients)
x_fit = np.linspace(min(x), max(x), 50)
y_fit = polynomial(x_fit)
```

```
plt.scatter(x, y, label='Data Points')
plt.plot(x_fit, y_fit, color='red', label='Best Fit Line')
plt.legend()
plt.show()
```

Exercise 4: Generate a histogram using random data.

```
# Generate random data
data = np.random.randn(1000)

plt.hist(data, bins=20)
plt.title('Random Data Histogram')
plt.xlabel('Data')
plt.ylabel('Frequency')
plt.show()
```

Keep plotting and exploring!

_ PIP Package Manager

The PIP Package Manager is Python's default package manager and stands for "Pip Installs Packages" or "Pip Installs Python." This handy tool makes installing, uninstalling, and managing Python packages a breeze. PIP is particularly useful for developers as it allows for quick package management via the command line. Installing a package is as simple as running `pip install package_name`. Similarly, to uninstall a package, you'd run `pip uninstall package_name`. PIP is versatile; you can even upgrade packages, list installed packages, and much more. It's a critical tool that every Python programmer should get comfortable with as it significantly streamlines the process of setting up your development environment and managing dependencies.

_ The Sys Module

The `sys` module in Python provides access to some variables used or maintained by the interpreter and to functions that interact strongly with the interpreter. It allows you to access system-specific parameters and functions, making it possible to do things like command line parsing, file I/O, and even system exit. Common uses of the `sys` module include `sys.argv` for command-line arguments, `sys.exit()` to exit a Python script, `sys.stdin`, `sys.stdout` and `sys.stderr` for standard I/O operations. It's a valuable tool for Python programmers interested in dealing with system-related tasks in their code.

_ Scrapy

Scrapy is an open-source web scraping framework for Python, used to extract data from websites. Think of it as a powerful tool to collect structured data from the Internet, something that could be particularly useful for data analysis or machine learning. You can build Scrapy spiders, which are Python classes defining how a certain site (or a group of sites) will be scraped. Scrapy takes care of requesting the web pages and downloading the HTML content for further parsing and extraction. It's highly customizable and can handle a wide range of scraping tasks out-of-the-box.

Requests

The Requests library is another essential tool for any Python developer. With it, you can send all kinds of HTTP requests, something crucial for API integration, web scraping, or even automating login procedures for websites. It abstracts many of the complexities and ensures that you don't have to mess around with low-level network parameters. One of its most attractive features is that it allows for both simple and complex HTTP requests using methods like `get()`, `post()`, `put()`, and more. For example, to get the content of a web page, you'd do `requests.get(url)` and you're done!

Pygame

Pygame is a set of Python modules designed for writing video games. But don't let the 'game' part fool you; it can be used for a variety of multimedia software projects. It provides functionalities like creating windows, drawing shapes, capturing mouse events, and playing sounds. Pygame is highly portable and can run on nearly every platform and operating system. Whether you're a newbie trying to make your first game or a seasoned developer, Pygame offers a set of straightforward functionalities to bring your ideas to life.

Beautiful Soup

Beautiful Soup is a Python library designed for web scraping purposes to pull the data out of HTML and XML files. This library creates parse trees that can be used to extract data easily. Beautiful Soup automatically converts incoming documents to Unicode and outgoing documents to UTF-8. It sits on an HTML or XML parser and provides Pythonic idioms for iterating, searching, and modifying the parse tree. Whether you're a data scientist who needs to scrape thousands of e-commerce reviews, or a developer who needs to parse an XML configuration file, Beautiful Soup is incredibly efficient and easy to use.

Pillow

Pillow is a powerful library for handling image files in Python. It's a modern version of PIL (Python Imaging Library) and is maintained by the same community. It supports various image file formats like PNG, JPEG, and TIFF. The library provides a wide array of image processing capabilities including filtering, cropping, rotating, and color manipulation. So if you're looking to build an application that involves image editing or simply want to automate the process of manipulating images, Pillow is a great tool to have in your toolbox.

TensorFlow

TensorFlow is an open-source machine learning library developed by researchers and engineers from the Google Brain team. It's one of the most popular libraries for implementing machine learning algorithms and is very well-suited for deep learning. With a flexible architecture, TensorFlow allows for easy deployment of computation across a variety of platforms (CPUs, GPUs, TPUs), and from desktops to clusters of servers to mobile and edge devices. It has a rich ecosystem of tools, libraries, and community resources that lets researchers push the state-of-the-art in ML, making it an excellent choice for both academic and industrial research.

Scikit-Learn

Scikit-learn is a machine learning library in Python that provides simple and efficient tools for data analysis and data mining purposes. It's built on top of two essential Python libraries, NumPy and SciPy.

Scikit-learn supports various machine learning models including classification, regression, clustering, and dimensionality reduction. It also has built-in functions for model selection and evaluation, pre-processing, and more, making it a versatile tool for data scientists and machine learning engineers alike.

_ SciPy

SciPy is an open-source Python library used for scientific and technical computing. It builds on NumPy by adding a large number of higher-level algorithms for integration, ordinary differential equation solvers, and optimization algorithms. It's widely used in the field of scientific computing together with other libraries like Matplotlib for plotting and Pandas for data manipulation.

Would you like me to continue with the remaining topics?

_ Keras

Keras is an open-source deep learning API written in Python. It's known for its simplicity and ease of use, making it a great choice for beginners and experts alike. Built on top of TensorFlow, CNTK, or Theano, Keras provides a high-level, more intuitive set of abstractions that make it easy to develop deep learning models. It comes with built-in support for multi-GPU data parallelism and a variety of advanced layers and optimizer algorithms, empowering developers to focus more on the problem and less on the technical details.

_ Theano

Theano is another open-source numerical computation library that allows you to efficiently define, optimize, and evaluate mathematical expressions involving multi-dimensional arrays. While not specifically designed for machine learning, Theano is popularly used for deep learning applications and has inspired the architectural foundations of other more focused libraries, like TensorFlow. Though it's seen a decline in updates and community engagement compared to TensorFlow and PyTorch, it remains an important part of the machine learning ecosystem.

_ Twisted

Twisted is an event-driven networking engine written in Python. It's used for implementing network protocols, including clients, servers, and everything in-between. Whether you're building a web server, client, a system for real-time analytics, or a chatbot, Twisted is versatile enough to manage your network communications. It also has built-in support for many common network protocols, which you can extend and modify to fit custom networking requirements.

Chapter 13: Version Control System – GitHub Intro

GitHub is a version control system that has become the de facto standard for open-source projects. It's a crucial tool for Python developers to manage versioning, collaboration, and documentation of code. GitHub is not just a storage facility for your code but also provides a range of tools to streamline the coding process. These include pull requests for code reviews, issues for bug tracking and feature requests, and Actions for automated testing and deployment. If you're coding in Python, understanding how to use GitHub will go a long way in managing your projects efficiently. GitHub isn't just a place to store your code; it's a platform that offers various tools and community features that can help you grow as a Python developer. Here are some key aspects that a beginner should know:

Why GitHub?

1. Version Control: GitHub uses Git for version control, allowing you to keep track of changes, collaborate with other developers, and work on different features simultaneously without disturbing the main codebase.

2. Collaboration: GitHub provides a centralized location for your code, making it easier for other developers to collaborate with you. You can also contribute to other people's projects, making it a vibrant community of developers.

3. Open-Source Culture: Many Python libraries and frameworks are open-sourced on GitHub. This allows you to look under the hood, understanding how professionals write code and giving you an opportunity to contribute.

Basic Concepts

1. Repository: This is your project's folder where all your code files, documentation, and other assets live.

2. Clone: Downloading a repository from the remote server to your local machine.

3. Commit: Saving your changes to the local repository.

3. Push: Uploading your committed changes from your local repository to the remote server.

4. Pull: Downloading and integrating changes from the remote server to your local repository.

5. Branch: A separate instance of the codebase, where you can work on a specific task without affecting the main or other branches.

6. Pull Request: A method to submit your changes for review. Once reviewed and approved, they can be merged into the main codebase.

Getting Started

1. Create a GitHub Account: It's free for public repositories.

2. Install Git: Download and install Git on your machine.

3. Set Up Your Repository: Create a new repository on GitHub and clone it to your local machine to start adding your Python code.

4. Basic Git Commands: Familiarize yourself with basic Git commands like git add, git commit, git push, and git pull.

4. README and Documentation: Always include a README file to explain what your project is about, how to set it up, and how to use it.

5. Licenses: Understand basic licensing norms. If you want others to use your code, include an open-source license.

Chapter 14: Testing and Debugging

_ *Intro*

As you dive deeper into the programming universe, you're likely to encounter a few bumps along the road. Maybe your code isn't running as expected, or perhaps you're dealing with weird bugs that seem to appear out of nowhere. Welcome to the inevitable world of testing and debugging! We'll explore various techniques to ensure that your Python code not only works but works well.

Why Testing and Debugging?

First things first—why do we even need to test or debug our code?

1. Quality Assurance: Testing helps ensure your code does what it's supposed to do. Imagine deploying an application that hasn't been thoroughly tested. Users could run into numerous issues, leading to poor user experience and potentially tarnishing your project's reputation.

2. Easy Maintenance: Debugging and proper documentation make it easier to understand the ins and outs of the code. This is especially crucial when you're working with a team or when you revisit an old project after some time.

3. Reduce Future Errors: A good set of tests can serve as a safety net, helping you catch errors before your users do. Every time you add a new feature or refactor your code, running your test suite can alert you to any broken or regressive functionality.

What's in this Chapter?

1. Writing Your First Test with Unittest: We'll kick things off by learning how to write your first unit test in Python using the built-in unittest framework.

2. Debugging Techniques and Tools: The chapter will introduce you to several Python debugging tools and techniques to help you track down those pesky bugs efficiently.

3. Effective Logging and Documentation: Logging isn't just for lumberjacks! We'll discuss how proper logging and documentation can save you hours of debugging time and how it's a critical part of any serious programming project.

_ *Writing Your First Test with Unittest*

Before we go hunting for software glitches, let's talk about setting traps to catch them before they cause chaos. That's right, I'm talking about unit testing. A unit test is essentially a code snippet that verifies if a specific part of your code is working as intended. These tests are like a safety net for developers, catching errors before they escalate into larger issues or make it into the final product.

Getting Started with Unittest

Python's standard library comes equipped with a testing framework called `unittest`. This testing library is inspired by Java's JUnit and is part of Python's standard utility modules.

To start, you'll need to import the `unittest` library. Then, define a test case class that inherits from `unittest.TestCase` and write test methods within it.

```
import unittest
```

```
class TestMyFunction(unittest.TestCase):

    def test_addition(self):
        self.assertEqual(add(1, 1), 2)

    def test_subtraction(self):
        self.assertEqual(subtract(2, 1), 1)
```

In this example, the `TestMyFunction` class inherits from `unittest.TestCase`. We then define two test methods: `test_addition` and `test_subtraction`. These methods use `unittest`'s `assertEqual` function to validate the output of our fictional `add` and `subtract` functions.

Running Tests
To run your test suite, you can simply navigate to your test file's directory and execute:

```bash
bashCopy code
python -m unittest test_file_name.py
```

Replace `test_file_name.py` with your actual test file's name. If everything's hunky-dory, you'll see an output saying that your tests passed.

Test Fixtures: setUp and tearDown
The `unittest` framework also provides the `setUp` and `tearDown` methods. These methods allow you to set some initial conditions for your tests (`setUp`) and to clean up resources afterward (`tearDown`).

```
class TestMyFunction(unittest.TestCase):

    def setUp(self):
        print("Setting up resources")

    def tearDown(self):
        print("Cleaning up")
```

_ Debugging Techniques and Tools
Debugging is the Sherlock Holmes work of coding—it's about gathering clues to understand what's really going on with your program. It's a skill that, once mastered, will save you countless hours of hair-pulling and keyboard smashing.

Using Print Statements (The Old-School Way)
Before diving into sophisticated debugging tools, let's mention the classic but effective `print` statements. It's like the flashlight of debugging: basic but can show you what's in the dark corners of your code.

```
def mysterious_function(x):
    result = x * 2
    print(f"The result is {result}")
```

146

```
    return result
```

Using Python's Built-in Debugger (pdb)

Python comes with its built-in interactive debugger known as `pdb`. To drop into the interactive debugging session, just add `import pdb; pdb.set_trace()` in your code.

```python
def another_mysterious_function(x):
    import pdb; pdb.set_trace()
    result = x * 2
    return result
```

Here you can execute your code line-by-line (use 'n' and press Enter), inspect variables ('p variable_name'), and even change them on the fly!

IDE Debuggers

Most Integrated Development Environments (IDEs) like PyCharm, Visual Studio Code, or Eclipse provide sophisticated debugging tools. You can set breakpoints, watch variables, and even visualize the program's flow.

Logging: More Than Just Print

The logging library in Python offers a robust way to capture the state of your code at various points in time. Unlike `print` statements, logs can be configured to include additional information like timestamps, log levels (ERROR, DEBUG, INFO), and even file names and line numbers.

```python
import logging

logging.basicConfig(level=logging.DEBUG)
logging.debug("This is a debug message")
```

This way, you can filter out log messages based on their urgency or the component they belong to.

Exception Handling in Debugging

Never underestimate the power of good exception handling. A well-placed `try-except` block can give you valuable clues about why your code is misbehaving. More on this in the next chapter on Exception Handling.

Quick Recap

1. **Print Statements:** Quick and dirty.
2. **Python Debugger (pdb):** Powerful but requires familiarity with console commands.
3. **IDE Debuggers:** Offers graphical debugging features, great for beginners and experts alike.
4. **Logging:** For advanced, configurable messages.

The more you understand your tools, the quicker you'll solve the mystery.

Chapter 15: Projects and Practical Applications

Absolutely, keeping things beginner-friendly is the key here. Let's dive into our first project, which is creating a basic calculator.

Creating a Basic Calculator

In this project, we'll create a simple calculator that can perform basic arithmetic operations like addition, subtraction, multiplication, and division.

Tools and Libraries Needed

- Python (obviously!)
- A text editor (like Visual Studio Code, PyCharm, or even just Notepad)

Step 1: Set Up Your Development Environment

First thing's first. Make sure Python is installed on your computer. Open your text editor and create a new Python file, name it `basic_calculator.py`.

Step 2: Take User Inputs

We'll need two numbers from the user and an operator (like +, -, *, /). Here's how to get those.

```python
num1 = float(input("Enter the first number: "))
operator = input("Enter an operator (+, -, *, /): ")
num2 = float(input("Enter the second number: "))
```

Step 3: Perform Calculations

Now, we'll use simple `if-elif-else` statements to perform the calculation based on the user's input.

```python
if operator == "+":
    result = num1 + num2
elif operator == "-":
    result = num1 - num2
elif operator == "*":
    result = num1 * num2
elif operator == "/":
    if num2 != 0:  # We can't divide by zero
        result = num1 / num2
    else:
        result = "Undefined (can't divide by zero)"
else:
    result = "Invalid operator"

print(f"The result is: {result}")
```

Step 4: Run Your Program

Save the file and run it in the terminal by navigating to the folder where your `basic_calculator.py` is saved and type `python basic_calculator.py`.

And there you have it—a simple, yet functional calculator!

Absolutely, let's move on to the next project: Developing a Simple Web Scraper.

Developing a Simple Web Scraper

In this project, we will create a simple web scraper to fetch and display quotes from a website. We will be scraping quotes from `http://quotes.toscrape.com/`.

Tools and Libraries Needed

- Python
- Requests library (`pip install requests`)
- BeautifulSoup (`pip install beautifulsoup4`)

  - A text editor

Step 1: Install Required Libraries

Open your terminal and install the necessary libraries:

```
pip install requests beautifulsoup4
```

Step 2: Setup Your Development Environment

Create a new Python file, and name it `simple_web_scraper.py`.

Step 3: Import Libraries and Fetch Website Data

```python
import requests
from bs4 import BeautifulSoup

response = requests.get('http://quotes.toscrape.com/')
```

Step 4: Parse HTML Content

```python
soup = BeautifulSoup(response.text, 'html.parser')
```

Step 5: Scrape Quotes

We'll find all the quotes on the first page and print them out.

```python
quotes = soup.find_all('span', class_='text')

for quote in quotes:
```

```
    print(quote.text)
```

Step 6: Run Your Program
Save your Python file and run it in the terminal:

```
python simple_web_scraper.py
```

You should see a list of quotes printed to your terminal.

Great, let's dive into the next project: Crafting a GUI Application.

_ *Crafting a GUI Application*
The goal here is to create a simple Graphical User Interface (GUI) application that allows the user to perform basic text manipulations like converting text to uppercase, lowercase, etc.

Tools and Libraries Needed
- Python
- Tkinter library (pre-installed with Python)
- Text Editor

Step 1: Import Tkinter Library
Open a new Python file and name it `simple_text_manipulator.py`. First, import the Tkinter library.

```
from tkinter import *
```

Step 2: Create a Basic Window
Create the main window for the application.

```
root = Tk()
root.title('Simple Text Manipulator')
```

Step 3: Add a Text Box
Create a text box where users can enter text.

```
text_box = Text(root, height=10, width=40)
text_box.pack()
```

Step 4: Create Buttons and Their Functions
Create buttons to manipulate the text.

```
def to_uppercase():
    entered_text = text_box.get('1.0', 'end-1c')
    text_box.delete('1.0', END)
    text_box.insert('1.0', entered_text.upper())


uppercase_button = Button(root, text="Uppercase", command=to_uppercase)
```

```
uppercase_button.pack()
```

Repeat these steps to create other text manipulation options like lowercase, reverse text, etc.

Step 5: Run the Application
After adding all the buttons and functionalities, run the main Tkinter loop to display the application.

```
root.mainloop()
```

Save your file and run it in the terminal.

```
python simple_text_manipulator.py
```

You should see a window with a text box and buttons for text manipulation.

Fantastic, you're making excellent progress! Let's get into the next project, which is about building a simple chatbot.

_Building a Simple Chatbot
Create a basic chatbot that can respond to a handful of predefined queries. We'll use Python's built-in data structures for this one, so you won't need any special libraries!

Tools and Libraries Needed
- Python
- Text Editor

Step 1: Initialize Basic Data Structure
Create a Python dictionary to store some common questions and responses.

```
response_dict = {
    "hello": "Hi, how can I assist you?",
    "who are you": "I'm a simple chatbot.",
    "bye": "Goodbye!"
}
```

Step 2: Create the Chat Loop
Create a loop where the chatbot will look for the user's query in the dictionary and respond.

```
while True:
    user_input = input("You: ").lower()
    response = response_dict.get(user_input, "I don't understand that.")
    print("Bot:", response)

    if user_input == 'bye':
```

151

```
break
```

Step 3: Test the Chatbot
Run your script and interact with your chatbot in the console.

Step 4: Add More Complexity (Optional)
If you're feeling adventurous, you could expand your chatbot's vocabulary or integrate more complex decision-making logic.

Awesome, you're on a roll! The next project we're diving into is creating a simple weather dashboard.

Creating a Simple Weather Dashboard
Build a basic weather dashboard that fetches weather data for a given location using an API and displays it.

Tools and Libraries Needed
- Python
- Requests library for Python
- Text Editor
- API Key from a weather service (e.g., OpenWeather)

Step 1: Install Required Libraries
First, install the Requests library by running `pip install requests` in your command prompt or terminal.

Step 2: Fetch Weather Data
Here's a template for fetching weather data:

```python
import requests


def fetch_weather(location, api_key):
    url = f"http://api.openweathermap.org/data/2.5/weather?q={location}&appid={api_key}"
    response = requests.get(url)
    return response.json()
```

Step 3: Display Weather Data
Now, let's create a function to display the fetched data in a readable format.

```python
def display_weather(weather_data):
    print(f"Location: {weather_data['name']}")
    print(f"Temperature: {weather_data['main']['temp']} Kelvin")
    print(f"Description: {weather_data['weather'][0]['description']}")
```

Step 4: Connect All the Parts

Now, connect all the parts together in a main function.

```python
def main():
    location = input("Enter location: ")
    api_key = "YOUR_API_KEY_HERE"

    weather_data = fetch_weather(location, api_key)
    display_weather(weather_data)

if __name__ == "__main__":
    main()
```

Additional Challenges

Creating a Basic Calculator

Exercise: Add a feature that allows users to perform calculations with decimals (floating-point numbers).

Solution

You can change the input conversion from `int()` to `float()` to accommodate decimal numbers.

```python
first_number = float(input("Enter the first number: "))
```

Developing a Simple Web Scraper

Exercise: Modify the web scraper to collect and save images from a webpage.

Solution

You could use the BeautifulSoup library's methods to find image URLs, and then download and save them using the Requests library.

```python
img_url = soup.find('img')['src']
img_data = requests.get(img_url).content
with open('image_name.jpg', 'wb') as handler:
    handler.write(img_data)
```

Crafting a GUI Application

Exercise: Extend the application to include additional functionalities like a 'Clear' button.

Solution

You can add a button widget that, when clicked, clears all input and output fields.

```python
def clear_all():
    entry.delete(0, 'end')
    label.config(text = " ")
```

```
clear_button = Button(window, text="Clear", command=clear_all)
clear_button.pack()
```

Building a Chatbot

Exercise: Add a feature to your chatbot that allows it to remember past interactions during a session.

Solution

You can create a Python list to hold the history of interactions and display them when needed.

```
history = []

def remember_interaction(user_input, bot_output):
    history.append({"user": user_input, "bot": bot_output})

def show_history():
    for interaction in history:
        print(f"User: {interaction['user']}\nBot: {interaction['bot']}")
```

Creating a Weather Dashboard

Exercise: Convert the temperature from Kelvin to Fahrenheit or Celsius.

Solution

You can convert the temperature as follows:

- To Fahrenheit: `((temp_in_kelvin - 273.15) * 9/5) + 32`
- To Celsius: `temp_in_kelvin - 273.15`

```
def display_weather(weather_data):
    temp_k = weather_data['main']['temp']
    temp_f = ((temp_k - 273.15) * 9/5) + 32
    print(f"Temperature: {temp_f} Fahrenheit")
```

Chapter 16: Next Steps and Resources

Further Learning Paths: Advanced Topics and Specializations

You've dipped your toes into the world of Python and gotten a taste of what this powerful language can do. But remember, you've just scratched the surface! Let's talk about what comes next and how you can expand your Python skills to really make a splash.

Data Science and Machine Learning

If numbers are your thing, or you're just fascinated by all the buzz around data, dive deeper into Python libraries like NumPy, Pandas, and Matplotlib. You can also explore machine learning frameworks like scikit-learn and TensorFlow to build models and make predictions.

Web Development

If you love the idea of building your own websites or web applications, consider learning frameworks like Django or Flask. They'll make your life a lot easier, taking care of many of the nitty-gritty details.

Automation and Scripting

Python shines in automating repetitive tasks. From file management to network automation, Python can be your trusty sidekick, saving you tons of time. Look into libraries like Selenium or tools like Ansible.

Game Development

Believe it or not, you can make games with Python! With the help of libraries like Pygame, you can build everything from simple puzzles to complex interactive games.

Cybersecurity

Python can also arm you with the tools needed for ethical hacking. Libraries like Scapy or frameworks like Metasploit can help you understand security protocols and conduct penetration tests.

Natural Language Processing (NLP)

If you're intrigued by how machines understand human language, NLP is worth a shot. Python libraries like NLTK and SpaCy are commonly used in this field for tasks like sentiment analysis and chatbot development.

Mobile App Development

While Python isn't a traditional language for mobile development, frameworks like Kivy make it possible to create mobile apps using Python. These won't be as efficient as apps built with native languages but are a good start.

Hardware and IoT

Python's simplicity and readability make it a great choice for hardware programming and IoT (Internet of Things) applications. Libraries like RPi.GPIO allow for easy interface with hardware components.

Blockchain and Cryptocurrency

If you're interested in decentralized technology, Python has libraries for that too. You can build basic blockchain networks to understand how cryptocurrencies like Bitcoin work.

Specialization Courses and Certifications

To master these specializations, you can enroll in specific courses that give you a deep dive into these topics. Websites like Coursera, Udacity, and edX offer a range of courses that even come with certifications.

So, what will it be? The cool thing about Python is that you don't have to limit yourself to just one of these paths. The language is versatile enough to let you explore multiple avenues. Pick a project that excites you and take the plunge. The Python universe is vast, and there's room for everyone!

Joining the Python Community

Now that you've got your feet wet, let's talk about how you can become part of the larger Python community. Trust me, it's a warm and welcoming place, filled with people who are just as passionate about Python as you are.

Online Forums and Social Media

Places like Stack Overflow, Reddit's r/learnpython, and Twitter are buzzing with Python enthusiasts who share tips, answer questions, and discuss all things Python. Don't be shy—join in!

GitHub Repositories

Contributing to open-source projects on GitHub is a fantastic way to learn from experienced developers. It's like a virtual classroom where the projects are your textbooks. You can also find plenty of Python projects that are begging for some love and attention.

Python Conferences and Local Meetups

Whether it's PyCon, DjangoCon, or a local Python meetup, these events offer a chance to network, learn from experts, and even present your own projects. And don't worry if traveling isn't an option; many of these events are going virtual.

Online Courses and Webinars

Numerous online platforms offer Python courses that range from beginner to advanced levels. Webinars are also an excellent way to continue your Python education and keep up with the latest trends.

Blogs and Podcasts

There are countless Python-focused blogs and podcasts that offer valuable insights and tutorials. Following these can keep you updated and offer different perspectives on what you can do with Python.

Coding Challenges and Hackathons

Platforms like LeetCode and HackerRank offer Python-specific coding challenges that can test your skills. Hackathons are also a fun and intense way to collaborate on projects and solve real-world problems using Python.

Slack Channels and Discord Servers

Many Python-related communities maintain Slack channels or Discord servers where members share resources, offer advice, and discuss projects. These platforms often host Q&A sessions with Python experts and offer coding help.

Python Software Foundation (PSF)

The PSF is the organization behind Python, and they offer resources, sponsor events, and even provide grants for Python-related initiatives. You might consider becoming a contributing member.

Publish Your Own Work

As you gain confidence, consider publishing your projects and tutorials. Whether it's a simple script or a complex application, sharing your work contributes to the community and builds your profile.

Mentorship and Teaching

Once you're comfortable with Python, why not give back to the community by mentoring newbies or creating educational content? Teaching is a powerful tool for reinforcing your own knowledge.

Being part of a community can make your Python journey much more enriching. Not only do you learn faster, but you also get to share your triumphs and pitfalls with people who get it. So, go ahead, become part of the Python universe. It's a decision you won't regret!

Resources for Continuous Learning

There's a wealth of resources available to help you continue learning, and they're just a click away. Let's delve into some of these go-to resources you'll want to bookmark.

Online Documentation and Tutorials

The Python official website is your first stop. Their documentation is robust, offering guides, tutorials, and a wealth of examples. Websites like W3Schools, GeeksforGeeks offer great tutorials for all levels.

Python Official Website
URL: https://www.python.org/

The official Python website offers robust documentation that covers the language in depth. You'll find comprehensive guides, tutorials, and a ton of example code.

W3Schools
URL: https://www.w3schools.com/python/

W3Schools offers beginner-friendly tutorials and exercises. It is an excellent resource for those who are new to Python or programming in general.

GeeksforGeeks
URL: https://www.geeksforgeeks.org/python-programming-language/

GeeksforGeeks provides tutorials that are perfect for those who are beyond the beginner stage. They have articles and tutorials that dig into more complex subjects like data structures, algorithms, and more.

Blogs and Newsletters

Following blogs such as Towards Data Science, PyBites, and Dan Bader's Real Python can keep you in the loop about the latest Python developments. Newsletters like Python Weekly and Pycoder's Weekly are great for a quick read.

GitHub Repos

As mentioned earlier, GitHub is a goldmine for Pythonistas. Following trending repositories can give you insight into what's hot in the Python world right now.

Community Forums and Social Media Groups

Apart from the popular ones like Reddit and Stack Overflow, there are Python-focused groups on Facebook and LinkedIn where you can post queries, share resources, or just engage in general Python banter.

Open Source Projects

Contributing to or even just exploring open-source projects can be both educational and rewarding. Websites like Up for Grabs and First Timers Only can help you find projects that match your skill level.

Thank you!

Creating this book represented a journey fueled by dedication and our deep-seated passion for disseminating knowledge and skills that are pivotal in navigating our rapidly evolving, dynamic world. Your encouragement and support are not just appreciated – they are fundamental to our mission and inspire us to continue making meaningful contributions.

We are very happy that you have reached this far. Your feedback is invaluable to us, and we would greatly appreciate it if you could share your experience. Providing a review is simple, straightforward and will not take more than 1 minute: just scan the QR code provided below. Feel free to express yourself in a way that suits you best! How to?

Option A: Create a brief video review showcasing the book.

Option B: Prefer not to be on camera? No issue at all. You can opt to capture some photographs of the book or write just a brief textual review. Your insights are crucial, as they not only recognize our efforts but also assist others in discovering this resource.

Please note, while providing a review is entirely optional, your feedback is extremely important and valuable.

Scan the QR code below to leave your review

Thank you so much!

Retrieve Your Bonus Content

We strongly encourage you to take advantage of the valuable bonus content that accompanies this resource. These resources can facilitate and augment your comprehension throughout the entirety of the text. To access these supplementary scan the QR code or go to the link below

Scan the QR Code below to access your bonus content

Or got to the following link → rebrand.ly/py-extra

Thank you

Made in United States
Cleveland, OH
01 November 2024

10382399R00090